Channel Hopping

by Andrew Sanger

Andrew Sanger is a well-established contributor to the travel pages of British newspapers and magazines, and was editor of *Rail Europe* magazine from 1990 to 1999. He has written more than 20 guidebooks, mainly on France, and has twice been a winner in the Travelex Travel Writers' Awards.

Driving through a tree lined avenue in the Dordogne

AA Publishing

The Automobile Association would like to thank the following photographers and associations for their assistance in the preparation of this book.

CITÉ DE L'EUROPE 20; **DIGITAL VISION** 87b, 87c; **G WHITEMAN** 28
All remaining pictures are held in the Association's own library **(AA PHOTO LIBRARY)** with contributions from the following photographers: A KOUPRIANOFF back cover (a) Guild House in Brussels, 70, 72, 74a, 74b, 75, 76, 79, 81; R MOORE 3, 49, 50, 56, 58, 61, 62a, 62b, 63, 64, 66 87a; R MOSS 12, 15; T OLIVER 9, 13, 24, 29, 34; D ROBERTSON 10, 19a, 19b, 26, 35; C SAWYER front cover, back cover (c) restaurant, 5, 42, 44, 48, 52, 53, 55, 65; B SMITH back cover (d) Hotel de Ville in Calais, 17, 60; T SOUTER back cover (b) baguettes

Contributors
Copy editor
Nia Williams

Indexer
Marie Lorimer

Revision management
Apostrophe S Limited

Written by Andrew Sanger with additional material by Teresa Fisher, Sylvie Franquet, Anthony Sattin, Caroline Sunderland and Nia Williams.
Updated by Andrew Sanger

First Published 1999.
Reprinted 2001. Information verified and updated.
Reprinted Apr and Nov 2002.
Reprinted 2004. Information verified and updated.

Published by AA Publishing, a trading name of Automobile Association Developments Limited, whose registered office is Millstream, Maidenhead Road, Windsor, Berkshire SL4 5GD. Registered number 1878835.

Mapping produced by the Cartographic Department of Automobile Association Developments Limited.

A CIP catalogue record for this book is available from the British Library.

ISBN 0 7495 3933 X

Colour separation: Pace Colour Southampton
Printed and bound in Italy by Printer Trento S.r.l.

A01641

Contents

Travelling across the Channel as a foot passenger on the ferries is an easy and inexpensive option

About this Book

KEY TO SYMBOLS

- map reference to the maps found in the What to See section
- address or location
- telephone number
- opening times
- restaurant or café on premises or near by
- nearest underground train station
- nearest bus/tram route
- nearest overground train station
- ferry crossings and boat excursions
- tourist information
- facilities for visitors with disabilities
- admission charge
- other places of interest near by
- other practical information
- ➤ indicates the page where you will find a fuller description
- travel by air

This book is divided into sections to cover the six main Channel-hopping destinations: Calais, Boulogne,Le Havre, Dieppe, Cherbourg and Ostend. Each destination is broken up to give detailed information:

In Three Days
More sights and activities for those with plenty of time to explore both the town and the surrounding area.

A Tour from...
Drive and explore the countryside around each port.

What to See
Detailed information on all the best destinations in the area.

Where To...
Detailed listings of the best places to eat, drink, stay and shop.

In addition some destinations give additional information including the major highlights to see if you only have one day in the port, excursions to towns near by, and also directions for scenic walks if you have more time.

Practical Matters pages 86–91
A highly visual section containing essential travel information.

Maps
All map references are to the individual maps found in this guide.
For example, the waterside district of Kruispoort in Bruges has the reference 80 2C – indicating the page on which the map is located and the grid square in which the area is to be found. A list of the maps that have been used in this travel guide can be found in the index.

Prices
Where appropriate, an indication of the cost of an establishment is given by € signs:
€€€ denotes higher prices, **€€** denotes average prices, while **€** denotes lower charges.

Star Ratings
Most of the places described in this book have been given a separate rating:

✪✪✪	Do not miss
✪✪	Highly recommended
✪	Worth seeing

Introduction

Whether for shopping, a breath of foreign air or a combination of the two, it's fun to hop across the Channel. Faster sea crossings and the Channel Tunnel have made it easier than ever. Cherbourg is less than three hours away by 'fastcraft', while the crossing to Calais is a mere 50 minutes.

Drive out of the terminal and big indoor shopping complexes and hypermarkets are waiting close by, with large car parks, a fantastic choice of things to buy, and often with eating places all under the same roof. Cité de l'Europe at Calais is the premier example. If you prefer town-centre shopping, colourful markets and tempting specialist cheese shops, bakers, cakemakers and *chocolatiers*, follow the signs for *Centre-Ville*. Boulogne and Dieppe, for example, are ideal.

Yes, there *is* more to life than shopping. Eating and drinking are the number one reason for a short break in France. Excellent restaurants are recommended in each of the ports and the countryside nearby. Try the cheeses, fish and creamy sauces of Normandy in and around Dieppe, Le Havre and Cherbourg. If you are a beer connoisseur, or would like to become one, head straight to Ostend and Bruges to sample some of Belgium's *six hundred* brews – that should take more than a weekend.

There are major family attractions at the Channel ports too, such as Boulogne's Nausicaa, one of the world's leading sea life centres. Reconnected to Dover in 2003 by a direct fast catamaran service, Boulogne is also less than 30 minutes' drive from Calais.

For those who want to go sightseeing, the Channel ports are well placed, each within a short drive of historic sights and picturesque countryside. None can beat Bruges, one of Europe's most treasured medieval jewels, just minutes away from Ostend.

Historic Mont-St-Michel has narrow walkways to explore

A 72-hour tour through the best of the region surrounding each port has been included – a treat for anyone who wants to escape the crowds and get deep into the 'real' France or Flanders. It might be only 72 hours, but you'll come home from a hop with more than a bootfull of bargains.

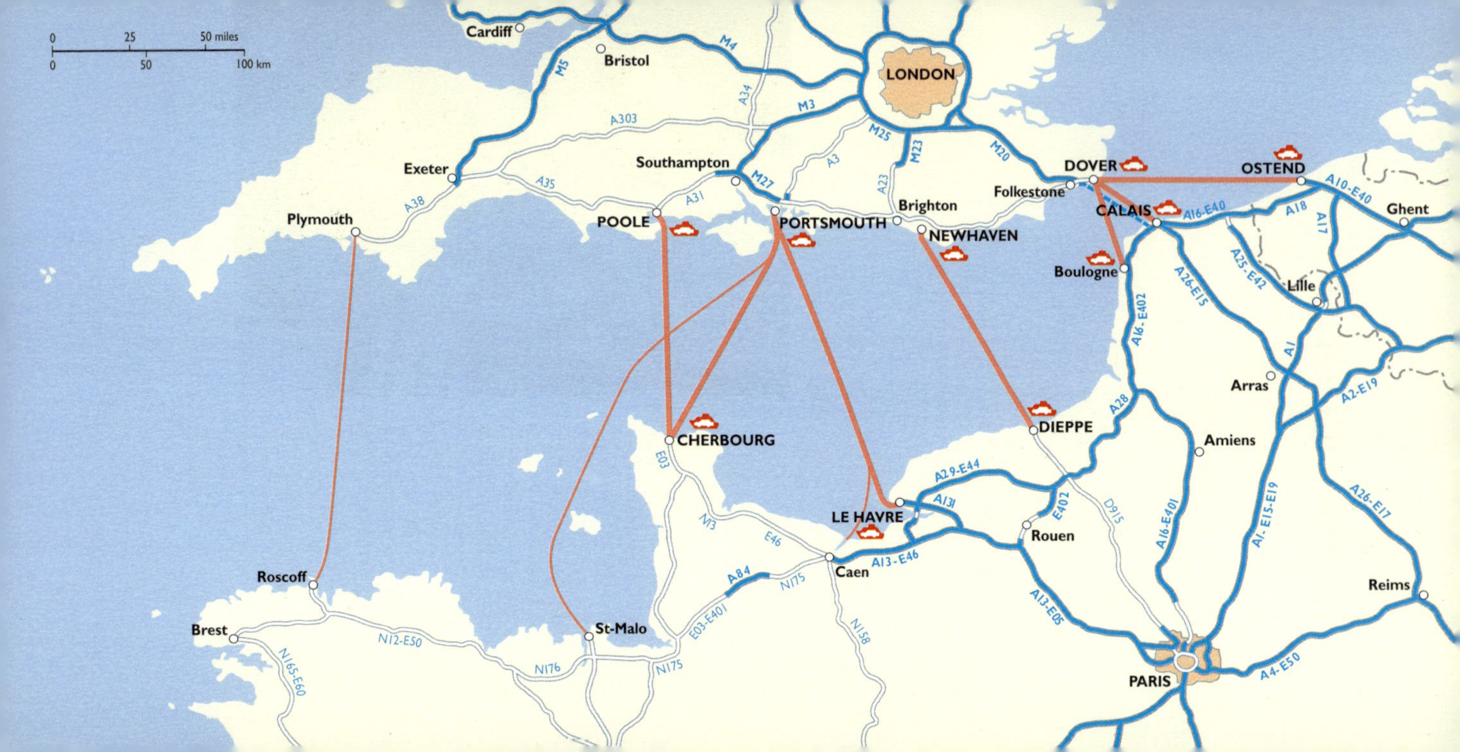
0 25 50 miles
0 50 100 km
Cardiff
Bristol
LONDON
Exeter
Plymouth
Southampton
POOLE
PORTSMOUTH
Brighton
NEWHAVEN
Folkestone
DOVER
OSTEND
CALAIS
Boulogne
Ghent
Lille
Arras
Amiens
DIEPPE
CHERBOURG
LE HAVRE
Rouen
Caen
Reims
PARIS
Roscoff
Brest
St-Malo
M5
M4
M3
M25
M23
M20
M27
A34
A303
A35
A38
A31
A3
A23
A10-E40
A18
A17
A16-E40
A25-E42
A26-E15
A16-E402
A1
A2-E19
A28
A29-E44
A131
E402
D915
A16-E401
A1-E15-E19
A26-E17
A4-E50
A13-E05
A13-E46
E46
N13
E03
A84
N175
E03-E401
N158
N12-E50
N176
N165-E60

Calais

Getting there

Calais is the Channel's best served passenger vehicle gateway into France. Several operators run car ferries from Dover to Calais with a combined frequency of about 60 return crossings daily. The journey takes 75–90 minutes. There are up to 15 crossings daily each way by fast catamaran from Dover (60 minutes). Trains take cars and passengers through the Channel Tunnel on the half hour journey with 1–4 departures per hour, day and night.

Arriving in Calais

Whether you travel by ferry or tunnel, you arrive a little out of town. In both cases, you drive out of the terminal onto a motorway (autoroute), with clear signs directing you either to Calais Town Centre ('Centre-Ville'), to Autoroute A16 (direction St-Omer, Reims) or Autoroute A26 (direction Boulogne to the south, Dunkerque and Lille to the north).

Calais in a Day

Most visitors to Calais come to shop. The Cité de l'Europe complex, 5km south of town towards Boulogne and close to the Eurotunnel terminal, is most convenient. La Cité, as locals call it, is a major shopping complex serving the whole Calais and Boulogne region, and it is as popular with residents as tourists. The shops range from budget to luxury and eating places include fast-food outlets as well as authentic restaurants with good food and wine. There is extensive free parking and many shops accept sterling.

Allow at least two hours at Cité de l'Europe – perhaps a full day. It's not hard to find your way around the two-storey complex, but if you do get lost, the information desks have a free map. Those who prefer to wander in real streets and enjoy the atmosphere of Calais town centre may prefer to do their shopping in town.

• **Head out to the Cité de l'Europe indoor shopping complex.** This huge commercial centre, near the Eurotunnel terminal, is the place for shopping sprees in any weather.

• **Lunch or dine at Cité de l'Europe or in one of the town's excellent brasseries.** La Cité contains a wide variety of eating places, but a town brasserie offers a more traditional setting.

• **Get orientated at place d'Armes.** This square, not far from the ferry port, is the main landmark of Calais-Nord, the older part of town, ringed by waterways. It has bars and brasseries, and is dominated by a brick watchtower, the Tour de Guet.

• **Stroll along rue Royale.** This is the main street from place d'Armes, through Calais-Nord, with hotels, restaurants and quality shops. At the end, cross the canal to the Town Hall.

• **Don't miss Rodin's famous sculpture.** Rodin was moved by the story of six local notables who offered to sacrifice themselves to save the town (➤ 16). His memorial stands outside the ornate Town Hall.

• **Window-shop in boulevard Jacquard.** This is the centre of modern Calais. Here are pâtisseries, *charcuteries* and other shops, as well as bars and brasseries.

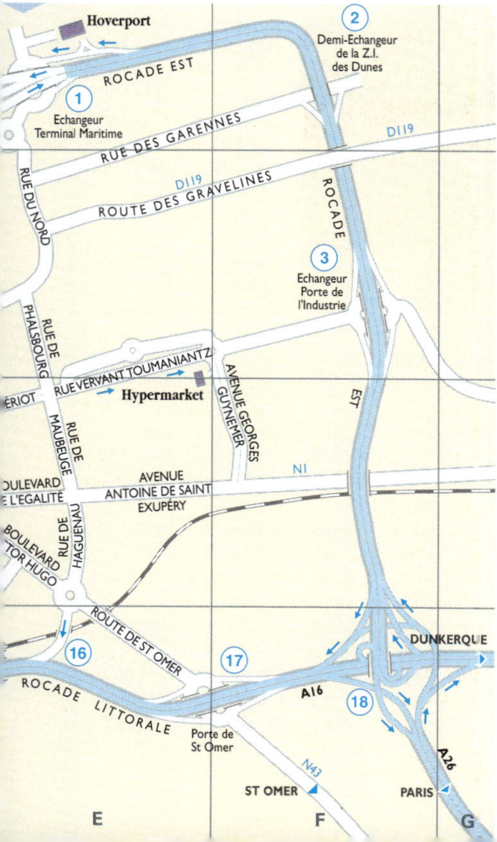

The Clock Tower on the Town Hall in Calais is one of the town's most well-recognised features

Calais in Three Days

Calais should be seen as a starting point rather than a destination. Day-trippers will find plenty to pass the time in Calais or at the out-of-town Cité de l'Europe shopping complex, but those with more time to spare should explore the interesting towns and villages inland and down the coast.

• **Go shopping at Cité de l'Europe,** the enormous indoor complex near the Calais Eurotunnel terminal, for food, wine, kitchenware, clothes and souvenirs.

• **Look around Calais town centre.** Window-shop along rue Royale, from place d'Armes to the Town Hall. This is the main street of Calais-Nord, the older part of town. Visit the town's museums of Fine Arts and Lace in rue Richelieu, and of the The War, in Parc St-Pierre. See Rodin's *Monument to the Burghers of Calais*; standing outside the Town Hall, this is Rodin's fine memorial to the self-sacrificing notables of the town. Pause in the Parc: well-tended Parc St-Pierre at the end of rue Royale is a haven of tranquillity where locals come for a stroll, a chat or a few moments' peace. Walk down boulevard Jacquard, the town's principal shopping street, and see what bargains are available.

The memorial at Vimy Ridge commemorates the sixty thousand Canadian troops who died here in just one battle during World War I

• **Lunch in town.** There are many inexpensive brasseries and restaurants along boulevard Jacquard, rue Royale and in place d'Armes.

• **Drive out to Cassel.** An interesting afternoon drive takes you from Calais to Cassel via the fortified village of Bergues and back via St-Omer, the Forest of Rihout-Clairmarais, Ardres and Guînes.

• **Eat out in a handsome Flemish town.** There are restaurants at Cassel, Bergues and St-Omer.

• **Visit Arras.** The quick way there and back is on Autoroute A26, all the way from Calais. Come off at Junction 7. The town deserves a visit of several hours and also has some good bars and restaurants.

• **Visit Vimy Ridge.** The World War I Canadian Memorial is close to Arras on Autoroute A26, just north of junction 7. The astonishing sight of its wartime trenches and battlefields gives a powerful insight into the events of the Great War, and creates unforgettable impressions.

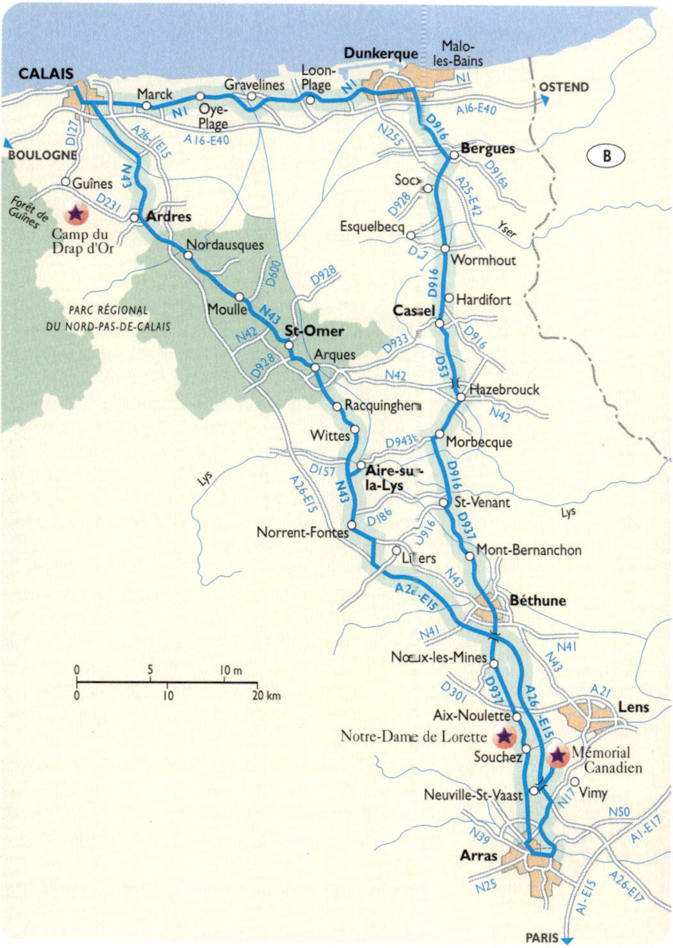

- **Drive the Opal Coast road to Boulogne.** The journey takes under an hour, passes through fishing villages and gives great clifftop views across the Channel to Kent.
- **Stroll around Boulogne's Old Quarter.** Calais' neighbouring port down the coast preserves more of its historic charm, especially the walled Haute Ville with its park-like ramparts walk.
- **Visit Nausicaa,** the huge Sea Life Centre at Boulogne. One of the best aquariums in the world, it takes several hours to visit. It also has a good restaurant.
- **Take time to head out of town,** for example down the Opal Coast as far as the seaside resort of Wissant. There are modest restaurants there, suitable for lunch or dinner.

A Tour from Calais

Distance
About 220km

Time
72 hours

Start/End Point
Calais

Tourist Information Offices

Calais
✉ 12 boulevard G. Clémenceau

Dunkerque
✉ 1 place Beffroi, rue de l'Amiral Ronarc'h

Arras
✉ place des Héros

St-Omer
✉ 4 rue du Lion d'or

Bergues
✉ place de la République

Cassel
✉ Grand'Place

Ferry to Dunkerque:
Norfolk Line operates a ferry direct from Dover to Dunkerque. The crossing takes 2 hours

It is worth taking a detour off the route to see the gardens of the château in Esquelbecq

Note that the 72-hour tour from Boulogne (► 29–33) passes through Calais and could also be done just as easily from Calais if preferred.

*Leave **Calais** on the N1 towards **Dunkerque**.*

As you drive to this large industrial port, note the typical Flemish watergangs – reclaimed marshland with a grid of drainage channels – beside the road. Dunkerque looks unappealing at first, but at the heart of the ring of refineries and factories there's a likeable old Flemish town. It has excellent shops and eating places, and few visitors.

The town's old fishing port is an easy place to park, and from there it's just five minutes on foot to the town centre, passing the ornate Town Hall on the way. The town's lively main square, place Jean Bart, is named after the terrifying 17th-century Dunkerque privateer who became one of the richest and most feared pirates of his time.

For many British visitors, Dunkerque is synonymous with the massive escape by Allied forces from the powerful German advance into northern France and Belgium in May 1940. Fleeing for their lives, Allied troops converged upon Dunkerque and boarded a huge flotilla of tiny vessels that took them back to Britain. From the town's harbour and the beach of neighbouring Malo-les-Bains over 350,000 Allied soldiers escaped. The story is told in the Fine Arts Museum (☎ 03 28 59 21 65) in place du Général de Gaulle. The town's two main landmarks are close by: the neo-Gothic church of St Eloi and Le Beffroi, the immense brick belfry, with the tourist office inside.

*Take the main road (D916) out of town in the direction of Cassel and Lille. After 7km, follow 'Centre-Ville' signs into **Bergues**.*

This pleasant town seems hardly to warrant the extraordinary, invincible rings of defences that surround it. Within the imposing fortified gateways, there are cobbled streets, elaborate flower-decked Flemish mansions and a fine 16th-century Town Hall and belfry.

*Return to the D916 and follow it to Cassel. On the way, you could take an interesting deviation through the village of **Esquelbecq**, on the right of the road. Reaching **Cassel**, follow 'Centre-Ville' signs up the hill into town.*

On a surprisingly high hill in this low Flanders landscape, Cassel is a peaceful town of charm and history. The central square, Grand'Place, is surrounded by imposing steep-roofed houses with dormer windows. One of the most striking is the 16th-century Hôtel de la Noble Cour, with its carved stone façade. Inside, there's a local museum.

Beside the square, the vast Notre-Dame church is in typically Flemish Gothic style. From here, steep, narrow back streets climb – sometimes in steps – to the summit of the hill, where a working 18th-century windmill stands in public gardens with an immense view of the farms, water-towers and steeples of Flanders.

Descend the steep hill onto little D53, following signs to ***Hazebrouck****. Leave Hazebrouck in the direction of Béthune on the D916. At a fork after the village of* ***St-Vénant****, take the D937 to* ***Béthune****. Drive through town, staying on the D937, and take the direction for Arras. Pass the Great War French National Cemetery, Notre-Dame de Lorette, on a high crest beside the village of* ***Souchez****, and take the D51 on the left to the Canadian Memorial,* ***Vimy Ridge****.*

One of the worst bloodbaths of World War I took place here, as Canadian troops tried to capture this strategic height. Sixty thousand Canadians died in a single battle on 9 and 10 April 1917 – the bodies of over 11,000 of them were never found. Part of the site has been maintained exactly as it was in 1919, while part has been allowed to weather and fade, giving a powerful sense of time passing. The maintained area, complete with trenches and tunnels, brings home forcefully the horrors of trench warfare. At the top of the ridge (Hill 145, as it was known during the war), a tall, sombre memorial gazes across the surrounding bleak mining landscape.

Take any of the signposted routes for the short drive into ***Arras****, on the D55, N17 or D937.*

The historic centre of Arras, a prosperous medieval market town, packed with grandiose Flemish architecture, had to be extensively rebuilt after both world wars. The centre of town is made up of two big cobbled squares surrounded by tall terraces of ornate, gabled, arcaded buildings. The larger of the two squares is the huge Grande Place, with the smaller place des Héros adjoining on its southwest corner. The smaller square contains the superb Town Hall, painstakingly restored to its original 16th-century style

Underneath the cobblestones, there's an extraordinary network of atmospheric tunnels and rooms called Les Souterrains. Entered from the Town Hall, they have been providing the people of Arras with shelter and refuge for over 1,000 years. The Arras Memorial to the Missing records the names of over 36,000 soldiers whose bodies were not found after World War I battles in this area, while

Running away to Calais

In the days before tourism and day trips, Calais and Boulogne were favourite bolt-holes for the well-to-do who had reason to get away from the public eye. Many were seriously in debt. Lady Hamilton, Nelson's mistress, died penniless in Calais at 27 rue Française, in 1815.

Take the opportunity to explore a local market – this one is at Arras

the Mur des Fusillées (Wall of the Shot) is where 200 French Resistance members were executed by the Germans in World War II.

Head on to the Arras ring-road and follow signs for the N17 (direction Lens, Lille) and A26 (direction Calais). Leave town on the N17 and, on reaching the junction with the A26, go on to the autoroute (direction Calais). Leave the autoroute at Junction 5 for ***Aire-sur-la-Lys****. Follow 'Centre-Ville' signs to the main square.*

Pause in Aire-sur-la-Lys, a busy market town. Standing at the meeting point of the River Lys and two canals, it's full of waterways. The centre of town is a huge cobbled triangular 'square', Grand'Place, dominated by an ornate balconied Town Hall, decorated with flowers and flags. Behind it rises the town's tall belfry. All around Grand'Place, narrow houses with steep roofs give masses of Flemish character, and among them you'll find useful bars and restaurants.

Away from the main square, St-Pierre Collegiate Church is easy to find thanks to its imposing 55m-high tower. It's one of the most interesting and important examples of Flemish Gothic – rebuilt in that style in the 15th century, when Flanders' wealth and cultural influence was at its highest, and faithfully reconstructed in the same style in 1944 after war damage.

Leave town on the N43, following signs to ***St-Omer****.*

Though a large, modern town, at its heart St-Omer has plenty of charm and hangs on to memories of Flanders. Flamboyant Flemish architecture surrounds the main square, place Foch. The most striking buildings include the Ancien Bailliage and Hôtel Sandelin. Here, too, is the wonderfully elaborate Town Hall (tourist office inside), so characteristic of the region. The town's great landmark is the 13th-century Gothic basilica of Notre-Dame. Huge inside, it contains good sculpture and, more interestingly, an astronomical clock dated 1558.

Take the D928 (direction Abbeville) to the D210 signposted Helfaut and ***La Coupole*** *(► panel), or return on the N43 (direction Calais) to* ***Ardres****.*

Ardres is a quiet, little town with few visitors. It has pretty corners and is well-placed for country walks and drives. Just 6km away, on the road to Guînes (D231), is the easily missed site of the Field of the Cloth of Gold (► 16). Beside it, Guînes Forest is lovely woodland with marked footpaths.

Continue into ***Calais*** *from Ardres on the N43, or go via* ***Guînes*** *on the D127.*

Here for the beer

French beer was not invented for British bargain-hunters. This region of France has been renowned for its local varieties of beer for centuries, and even today there are hundreds of small breweries. Cross the border into nearby Belgium, and you'll find an even livelier beer-drinking tradition.

From the war to the moon

La Coupole is housed in the very rocket bunker from where Hitler planned to launch his attack on Britain. This incredibly moving museum hosts two remarkable audio-visual presentations. One shows rocket science from wartime weaponry to the Apollo mission; the other reveals daily life in occupied France, through thousands of home movies and family photographs. Unforgettable features include the story of a little girl from Calais and her journey to the concentration camps. Allow three hours and two visits.

- Near St-Omer
- 03 21 93 07 07
- Apr–Oct 9–7; Nov–Mar 10–6. Closed second week in Jan
- Restaurant on site
- Good
- Expensive

A Walk Around Cassel

Only 55km southeast from Calais, Cassel is worth a visit during one of its festivals. The most important is on Easter Monday, when models of the Reuze giants, who supposedly created Mont Cassel by dropping a lump of earth, are the centrepiece of a carnival.

Start by the Musée in place du Général de Gaulle and walk towards the Town Hall.

Immediately after the 17th-century house at No 12 there is a good view to the left through the Porte d'Aire.

Turn right up rue du Château and go through the Porte du Château to the public gardens.

On the right is the Monument des Trois Batailles, and fine views of the Mont des Récollets and the Mont des Cats. To the left is the southern viewing platform, where, on a clear day, you can see over 60km.

Follow the path behind the windmill to the northern viewing platform by the statue of Maréchal Foch.

Cassel once had many windmills for wheat, cereal and oil, but only one survives: Casteel Meulen. The original, 16th-century mill burnt down in 1911 and was replaced in 1947.

Beyond the statue, turn left down the cobbled path to place du Général Vandamme. Follow the square round to the left. Turn right into rue Bollaert le Gavrian (not marked) and almost immediately left down the narrow passage of rue des Remparts.

Rue des Remparts meanders between the gardens and houses on the southern edge of the village.

Cross rue de l'Infirmerie and rue d'Aire into chemin de Tilleul. Bear left immediately and continue to a bridge that crosses the path. Turn left up the cobbled path, then right into rue du Maréchal Foch. Follow the road to a right-hand bend by a stonemason's; then turn left.

As the track narrows you can see the 17th-century Eglise des Jesuites above you on the left.

Climb the cobbled steps to the square in front of the chapel and turn right, passing the Eglise Notre-Dame on your left. Walk down the slope to place du Général de Gaulle.

Distance
2.5km

Time
1¼ hours

Start/End Point
place du Général de Gaulle

Lunch
Cafés in main square

Flags outside the Hôtel de la Noble Cour, Cassel

What to See

Rodin's famous Monument to the Burghers of Calais *stands near the Town Hall*

AIRE-SUR-LA-LYS (➤ 14, TOUR)

ARRAS (➤ 13, TOUR)

BERGUES (➤ 12, TOUR)

BLÉRIOT-PLAGE ✪

This little beach resort on the edge of Calais is named after pioneer aviator Louis Blériot, who flew across the Channel in 30 minutes on 25 July 1909. The exact spot is marked by a monument 500m west of the town centre.

CALAIS ✪✪✪

Visible even from outside the town, Hôtel de Ville (Town Hall) is an ornate 20th-century building in 15th-century Flemish style. A stained-glass window depicts the departure of the English from Calais in 1558. Standing outside Calais Town Hall is a sculpture by Rodin, the Monument des Bourgeois de Calais. It was carved in 1895 to honour the six leading citizens of the town who offered their own lives if Edward III would spare the town, which he had threatened to destroy. Moved by their self-sacrifice, he spared them – and the rest of the town.

Musée de la Guerre (Museum of War) Located in Mako Bunker, a large German bunker in Parc St-Pierre, opposite the Town Hall, the museum records the horrors and injustices of the German occupation.

Musée des Beaux Arts et de la Dentelle (Fine Arts and Lace Museum) As well as a fascinating section devoted to the local craft of lace-making, on which Calais prospered for centuries, the museum has important collections of 16th to 20th-century painting and sculpture including works by Rodin and Picasso.

The Tour du Guet in place d'Armes is the only authentic relic of the town's history; its gaunt brick watchtower dates back to the 13th century.

Calais
Musée de la Guerre
- Parc St-Pierre
- 03 21 34 21 57
- May–Sep 10–6, Oct–Dec, Feb–Apr 11–5. Closed Jan. Last admission 45 mins before closing
- Good
- Moderate

Musée des Beaux Arts et de la Dentelle
- 25 rue Richelieu
- 03 21 46 48 40
- Wed–Mon 10–12, 2–5:30 (Sat till 6pm, Sun 2–6:30). Closed public hols
- Good
- Moderate. Free on Wed

CAMP DU DRAP D'OR (FIELD OF THE CLOTH OF GOLD) ✪

In 1520, Henry VIII and François I met here, between Ardres and Guînes, to discuss England's claim to the whole of this region of France. Intended as 'peace talks', the encounter degenerated into a contest of ostentation as the two monarchs tried to outdo each other in splendour and riches - hence the name. A simple stone monument marks the spot in gilt letters.

- 13km south of Calais

CASSEL (➤ 15)

CÔTE D'OPALE (OPAL COAST) ✪✪✪

The coastline between Calais and Boulogne is surprisingly rustic, with simple farming and fishing villages. Cap Blanc-Nez and Cap Gris-Nez are the highest of the lofty viewpoints looking out to sea. The coast road is the D940.

LA COUPOLE (➤ 14, PANEL)

DUNKERQUE (➤ 12, TOUR)

ESQUELBECQ ✪

This quiet village has a paved central square; Grand'Place preserves its strongly Flemish character, and has a fortified brick château beside the River Yser.

10km south of Bergues

HONDSCHOOTE ✪✪

In the midst of a completely flat landscape, Hondschoote is a charming Flemish country town. For centuries, it was a large, prosperous town with over 3,000 workshops producing huge quantities of the finest cloth. In the main square, the 16th-century church, Town Hall and manor house are elaborate remnants of those prosperous times.

11km east of Bergues

A selection of cafés in and near Grand'Place

LILLE (➤ 18–19)

NAUSICAA (➤ 34, BOULOGNE)

ST-OMER (➤ 14, TOUR)

STEENVORDE ✪

Two well-preserved windmills, one cylindrical and brick, the other square and wooden, stand near this likeable, workaday Flemish village. Once known for its tapestries, the place is now known for its dairy produce.

6km east of Cassel

VIMY RIDGE (➤ 13, TOUR)

WISSANT ✪✪

The name is Flemish for White Sand, and this Opal Coast fishing village lies beside a huge beach backed by dunes. The beach is so large that local fishermen have the unusual custom of towing their fishing boats from the seashore to the village by tractor. They park outside their homes, or in the village centre, and sell their catch from the deck.

16km southwest of Calais

Two small hotel-restaurants in the village serve lunch and dinner

Excursion to Lille

This detail from a building on the place de la République is typical of Lille

The nearest French city to the Channel coast is just over 100km from Calais. Once a wealthy town in Flanders, Lille was taken by France in the 17th century. It remains a centre of Flemish culture, with its own Franco-Flemish patois. If you want to travel around in the city, use the unusual metro, VAL, with its automatic unmanned trains. This is a major shopping city, with a huge indoor complex called Euralille, near the centre and the Eurostar/TGV station. In the heart of the old city, the narrow lanes of historic Vieux Lille have high-quality specialist shops, fashion boutiques and restaurants. The tourist information office can be found in the place Rihour ☎ 03 20 21 94 21.

Several Lille restaurants have won high acclaim, especially **Le Sébastopol** (✉ 1 place de Sébastopol ☎ 03 20 57 05 05) and the Art Deco **L'Huîtrière** (✉ 3 rue Chats Bossus ☎ 03 20 55 43 41). For popular bars and brasseries, look at place Général de Gaulle and the rue de Gand in Vieux Lille.

Good mid-range hotels can be found in Vieux Lille and the main squares, such as the **Grand Hôtel Bellevue,** where the young Mozart once stayed (✉ 5 rue Jean Roisin ☎ 03 20 57 45 64), **Mercure Royal** (✉ 2 boulevard Carnot ☎ 03 20 14 71 47) or the **Hôtel de la Paix** (✉ 46bis rue Paris ☎ 03 20 54 63 93).

What to See in Lille

CITADELLE ✪✪

✉ West of the town centre
☎ Tourist Office: 03 20 21 94 21 (to reserve place on tour)
🕒 Guided 2-hour visits May–Oct Sun at 3
Moderate

Considered the greatest masterpiece of the military architect Vauban, Lille's vast fortress was a vital frontier defence for the new northern border of France after it had seized the city and the Flemish territory now known as Pas de Calais in 1667. The citadel has been occupied by the military ever since. The extraordinarily complex structure, enclosing a pentagonal central stronghold, is surrounded by a protective canal and includes other water channels, which can be flooded for additional security. It was capable of complete self-sufficiency, with its own food stores, wells and tradesmen's shops.

HOSPICE COMTESSE ✪✪✪

✉ 32 rue de la Monnaie
☎ 03 28 36 84 00
🕒 Daily 10–12:30, 2–6 (Mon pm only). Closed public hols
Moderate

Founded in 1237 by Countess Jeanne de Flandres, this historic charity hospital on the edge of Vieux Lille was rebuilt in the 17th and 18th centuries. The 15th-century barrel-vaulted Salle des Malades (hospital ward) has a 17th-century chapel at one end, built so that the sick could attend church services without leaving their beds.

Place Général de Gaulle is Lille's main square

Many of the other rooms and halls, including the tiled kitchen and the nuns' dormitory, now house a museum of furnishings, chinaware and porcelain and artwork.

PALAIS DES BEAUX-ARTS

France's second national art collection, after the Louvre, has reopened following six years of rennovation. Apart from a celebrated range of works by the 17th-century Dutch and Flemish masters, treasures include two Goyas, renaissance bas reliefs and a fine impressionists gallery. The basement houses Vauban's original models of his citadelles and fortified towns of Northern France.

place de la République
03 20 06 78 00
Mon 2–6, Wed–Sun 10–6, Fri until 7
Excellent
Moderate

PLACE GÉNÉRAL DE GAULLE (GRAND'PLACE)

The city's main square and medieval marketplace is a vast, open space edged with bars and fine old mansions, and the astonishing Vieille Bourse, dating from 1652 – a leading example of the late Flemish Renaissance style. The Vieille Bourse stands around a lavishly carved and decorated arcaded courtyard, the rather unlikely setting for a little market of secondhand goods and flowers.

PLACE DU THÉÂTRE

The smallest and loveliest of the three interconnecting squares at the centre of Lille, place du Théâtre is overlooked on one side by the early 20th-century Opéra House, on which ornament and statuary seem to be climbing out of the walls, while on the other side of the square is the rear of the opulent Vieille Bourse building.

VIEUX LILLE

Tall, often grand old buildings line the narrow back streets of this historic quarter. Many date from the 17th century and have been handsomely restored. Especially impressive are rue de la Monnaie, rue de la Grande Chaussée and its continuation rue des Chats Bossus, leading to place du Lion d'Or and place Louise de Bettignies, near the Hospice Comtesse.

A strangely disguised loudspeaker outside the Lille Opera House

Where to Shop

If the main purpose of your trip is to shop for bargains or for French style, Calais makes it easy thanks to the large Cité de l'Europe centre 5 km from town. Look out for low-cost wines, spirits, champagne and beer, perfumes, cheese and other foods, high-quality kitchenware at low prices, latest fashions and baby clothes. All are good value in France. Calais, in particular, has excellent bargain outlets for drinks.

Low prices and a great range of products bring thousands of visitors to Cité de l'Europe every day

Cité de l'Europe

A major indoor shopping complex covering some 60,000 sq m, with parking for thousands of cars, over 150 shops and around 20 eating places. Parts of the interior are themed to resemble town squares in the south of France – place de Lisbonne has tables around a fountain and even a painted sky. Shops sell a range of products, including men's and women's fashions, lingerie, jewellery, chocolates and kitchenware. There is an enormous **Carrefour Hypermarket**, so big that staff get around on roller skates, discount perfumery **Bernard Marrionnaud**, with exceptional bargains, gift shops and a huge Tesco's drinks supermarket called **Tesco Vin Plus**, which has France's largest retail selection of wine from around the world (with prices shown in £ and €).

✉ Well-signposted at Coquelles, beside Autoroute A16, a few minutes' drive from the Eurotunnel terminal, about 5km from Calais town centre (direction Boulogne) ☎ 03 21 46 47 48 ⌚ Shops: Mon–Thu 10–8, Fri 10–9, Sat 9–8. Closed Sun (except a few shops at the Porte de l'Espagne entrance). Carrefour Hypermarket: Mon–Fri 9AM–10PM, Sat 8:30AM–10PM; closed Sun. Restaurants: daily, 10AM–midnight

Calais Town Centre

The main shopping district is boulevard Jacquard and round the corner in boulevard Lafayette, with a smaller shopping area around place d'Armes and along rue Royale. Along these streets many shops offer a range of clothes, kitchenware and foods including cakes, breads and cheeses. **Le Chais** (✉ 40 rue Phalsbourg) is a cash and carry-style drinks shop popular with locals, specialising mainly in French wines.

There are street markets at place Crêvecoeur (off boulevard Lafayette) on Thursday and Saturday mornings, and at place d'Armes on Wednesdays and Saturdays. Many smaller shops in Calais close on Monday.

Prisunic

City centre branch of the popular chain store and supermarket. Ideal for stocking up on the essentials if you do not have time to visit the edge of town hypermarkets.
✉ 17 boulevard Jacquard 🕐 Mon–Sat 8:30–7:30, Sun 10–7 (certain periods only)

Out of the Centre

Auchan (formerly Mammouth).
Huge, user-friendly hypermarket and other stores, including a pleasant Sainsbury's wine store **(Boutique Sainsbury's)**, which has probably the best – not the largest – selection of wines from around the world, and with prices marked in £ as well as €.
✉ Centre Commercial, Avenue Roger Salengro, route de Boulogne (N1) 🕐 Hypermarket: 8:30AM–10PM. Closed Sun. Sainsbury's: 8:30AM–9PM. Closed Sun

Carrefour

Large hypermarket, less appealing than Auchan, with similar range of products.
✉ Close to A26, Junction 3 🕐 Mon–Sat 8:30AM–9PM

Eastenders

The legendary, pioneering drinks warehouse aimed at the unpretentious British shopper. Very wide choice, good value for money.
✉ 14 rue Gustav Courbet, Calais 🕐 Daily 24 hours

Franglais Beer and Wine

Some buyers prefer this outlet for its location and its wide choice of mainly French wines, with tasting room.
✉ Near Calais Eurostar/TGV station at Fréthun 🕐 9–7 (6:30 on Sat), Sun 9:30–6

Pérardel

Noted for its top-quality restaurant in the Champagne region and its chain of wine supermarkets with higher quality French wines, and inexpensive champagnes.
✉ Rue Marcel Doret, Zone Industriel Marcel Doret, A 26 Junction 3 🕐 Daily 8:30–8

Wine and Beer World

British-owned, this is a big, attractive, warehouse-style wine and drinks outlet aimed at the booze-cruise market
✉ 1 rue Judée, Zone Industriel Marcel Doret, A 26 Junction 3; also Avenue Roger Salengro 🕐 Mon–Tue 7AM–10PM, Wed–Fri 7–12AM, Sat–Sun 7AM–10:15PM

Lille

The Sunday morning flea market at Wazemmes (🚇 Gambetta) is a bustling social event. In the old town many stylish boutiques and galleries offer scope for browsing. The modern Euralille mall by the Eurostar station has a huge *Carrefour* hypemarket. The town is also home to France's biggest bookshop, *Le Furet du Nord* on place de Gaulle.

Roubaix

Once home to the textile mills and factories of the north, Roubaix is now part of the Greater Lille metropolitan area and is a Mecca for clothes shopping. Of its various factory outlet centres, the pedestrianised **McArthur Glen** is where top brands sell at 30–40 per cent below usual prices and even lower during the January and July sales. From central Lille take the métro or picturesque half-hour tram journey to Euro-Téléport.
✉ 44 Mail de Lannoy ☎ 03 28 33 36 00 🕐 Mon–Sat 10–7; open some Sun and public hols

Where to Eat & Drink

Aire-sur-la-Lys

Les Trois Mouquetaires (€€–€€€)
A charming hotel-restaurant in lovely grounds with high-quality dining on regional and French dishes.
✉ Château de la Redoute ☎ 03 21 39 01 11 Ⓘ Closed 20 Dec–20 Jan

Arras

La Coupole d'Arras (€€)
A welcoming and popular place serving seafood.
✉ 26 boulevard de Strasbourg ☎ 03 21 71 88 44 Ⓘ Closed Sat lunch

La Faisanderie (€€€)
In a vaulted cellar of a grand old Flemish building, the restaurant offers exceptional, imaginative cooking.
✉ 45 Grand'Place ☎ 03 21 48 20 76 Ⓘ Closed Sun PM, Mon, school hols, Feb, 3–24 Aug

Bergues

Au Cornet d'Or (€€–€€€)
In the timbered, stylish interior of a delightful flower-decked 18th-century house; classic French.
✉ 26 rue Espagnole ☎ 03 28 68 66 27 Ⓘ Closed Sun PM, Mon, end of Jun

Bollezeele

Hostellerie St-Louis (€€–€€€)
Amiable, very competent service and cooking in this delightful country hotel, with excellent wine list (Monsieur le Patron is a master sommelier). Dinner only.
✉ 47 rue de l'Eglise ☎ 03 28 68 81 83 Ⓘ Closed 4–18 Jan, Feb, Sun PM

Calais and Coquelles

Aquar'Aile (€–€€)
A spacious restaurant with large windows overlooking the sea. Excellent service and high-quality fish dishes. Over 150 different whiskies.
✉ 255 rue Jean Moulin ☎ 03 21 34 00 00 Ⓘ Closed Mon, Sun PM

Le Channel (€–€€)
Grills, seafood and classic dishes served in a large restaurant with sea views.
✉ 3 boulevard du Résistance ☎ 03 21 34 42 30 Ⓘ Closed 2 weeks in summer

Cité de l'Europe (€–€€)
Well over a dozen eating places, including McDonald's, Flunch (for French-style fast food), pizzerias and brasseries.
✉ Coquelles, beside Autoroute A16, a few minutes' drive from the Eurotunnel terminal, about 5km from Calais Ⓘ Open daily 10AM–midnight

Côte d'Argent (€–€€)
A modern place with a view of the ferries; quality cooking with fish specialities.
✉ 1 Digue Gaston Berthe ☎ 03 21 96 42 10 Ⓘ Hours vary, call to check

La Diligénce (€–€€)
Local dishes and top-quality fresh seafood at a hotel-restaurant, quietly located near rue Royale.
✉ 5 rue Roche ☎ 03 21 34 57 03 Ⓘ Closed Sat lunch

George V (€–€€)
An old favourite with many British visitors, this good old-fashioned hotel-restaurant on the rue Royale caters for a range of tastes, from hearty grills to fine cuisine.
✉ 36 rue Royale ☎ 03 21 97 68 00 Ⓘ Closed Sat lunch and Sun, festivals, 23 Dec–4 Jan

Histoire Ancienne (€–€€)
Chef-proprietor Patrick Comte learned his skills at some of the top high-class hotel-restaurants around France, hence advance booking is essential if you want to eat at his traditional 1930s-style brasserie. Take a seat facing the fireplace and you'll be able to watch your food being grilled over the embers. It's also a highly rated 'traiteur' providing local people with take-away gourmet dishes.
✉ 20 rue Royale ☎ 03 21 34 11 20 Ⓘ Closed Sun, Mon PM

St-Omer

Le Vainquai (€€)
The restaurant of a quality, hotel, Le Bretagne, near Calais but far enough away to leave the crowds behind. Good, reliable classic French and Flemish cooking.
✉ 2 place du Vainquai ☎ 03 21 38 25 78 Ⓘ Closed Sat lunch, Sun PM

Where to Stay

Remember that it's worth staying out of town to find places with more character. All the hotels mentioned here are under an hour from Calais.

Aire-sur-la-Lys

Les Trois Mouquetaires (€€)

A lovely, friendly hotel in a 19th-century 'château' with beautiful grounds and top-quality restaurant.

Château de la Redoute

03 21 39 01 11

Closed 20 Dec–20 Jan

Bollezeele

Hostellerie St-Louis (€€)

Set in a rustic village in flat, Flemish farmland, this 18th-century mansion is a comfortable hotel with an excellent restaurant popular with locals for special occasions.

47 rue de l'Eglise

03 28 68 81 83

Calais and Coquelles

Le Copthorne (€€€)

Modern, well-equipped hotel with a pool, a health club, a good restaurant and other facilities, in peaceful woods close to Cité de l'Europe. A few minutes from the A16, Junction 12.

avenue Charles-de-Gaulle, Coquelles **03 21 46 60 60**

Formule 1 (€)

Part of a big, nationwide, budget chain, these unstaffed hotels are the cheapest option: rooms (sleep three) are tiny, but have a TV and shower and cost under £20. On the edge of town near Cité de l'Europe.

avenue Charles-de-Gaulle, Coquelles **03 21 82 67 00**

George V (€€)

This traditional, comfortable, good-quality hotel offers an acceptable standard at reasonable prices, has a good restaurant and is perfectly situated in the heart of Calais-Nord, the tourist area of town.

36 rue Royale

03 21 97 68 00

Holiday Inn Garden Court (€€€)

Convenient for ferry travellers, this friendly, modern, well-equipped hotel near the port has a gym, efficient service, a decent, inexpensive grill restaurant and good breakfasts.

boulevard des Alliés

03 21 34 69 69

Métropol Hôtel (€–€€)

In the centre of town, near the Town Hall, this traditional hotel has small, comfortable rooms and a pleasant bar.

43 quai du Rhin

03 21 97 54 00

Meurice (€€€)

Modern, three-star hotel in restored style of its 18th-century predecessor and furnished with genuine antiques, beside Parc Richelieu. One of the best hotels in Calais.

5 rue Edmond-Roche

03 21 34 57 03

St-Omer

Hôtel Château Tilques (€€€)

A very grand luxury hotel in a fine Flemish manor house in glorious parkland setting. Its restaurant is located in the former 17th-century stables.

Tilques, 5km from St-Omer

03 21 93 28 99

Le Bretagne (€€)

This centrally located mid-range hotel has a good moderately priced restaurant and a popular bar open till 1AM. There's English TV available in the rooms, and a good breafast buffet served in the lounge.

2 place du Vainquai

03 21 38 25 78

Boulogne

Getting there

For some three years until 2003, the once-busy port of Boulogne was without any direct cross-Channel service. However, its proximity to the Channel Tunnel terminal near Calais – some 20km away on Autoroute A16 – means that for motorists the journey time from the UK to Boulogne by Eurotunnel is about the same as by direct ferry or catamaran. In 2003 a new high-speed craft came into service operated by SpeedFerries, crossing from Dover to Boulogne in 50 minutes, with five return crossings daily.

Arriving

The port is alongside the town centre, which is clearly signposted for both pedestrians and motorists.

Enjoying café life in Boulogne

Boulogne in a Day

For charm, sightseeing and gastronomy, Boulogne has the edge over Calais. Or if you just want to shop, the town has high quality local stores as well as hypermarkets, and is under half-an-hour's drive from Cité de l'Europe.

The town beach is a great place to relax for a while

- **Shop in town.** There is great speciality shopping available at the excellent little stores in Boulogne's Ville Basse (Lower Town).
- **Pop into the tourist office.** It's on quai de la Poste, alongside the Liane river, and will provide you with helpful information about what to see in the town.
- **Walk to place Dalton.** You'll find this pleasant market square a few paces along Grande Rue. It makes an ideal spot for a second breakfast, a drink or some lunch, and on Wednesday and Saturday mornings is filled to the brim with

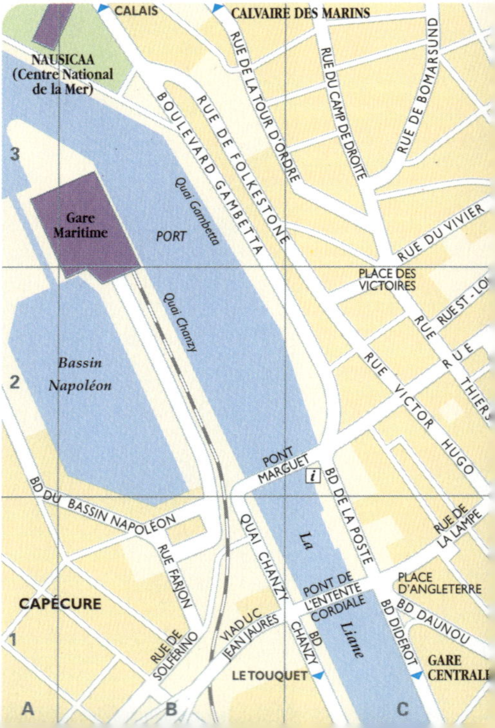

market stalls offering shoppers the best of local produce.

• **Stroll in the Ville Haute.** Walk up Grande Rue to the historic Ville Haute (Upper Town), where you'll find quiet, cobbled streets, and well-restored mansions. If it's time to eat, there are several good restaurants up here.

• **Visit the Basilique Notre-Dame.** This curious old domed structure is one of the landmarks of Boulogne.

• **Do the ramparts walk.** This old hilltop district is enclosed by high ramparts, with a wide, leafy walkway along the top. The walk around it, with extensive views, is a delight.

• **Visit Nausicaa.** The spectacular Sea Life Centre on the edge of town is one of the biggest and best in the world, popular with children and an enjoyable experience for adults, too. Allow several hours.

• **Walk by the sea.** Right beside Nausicaa is the town beach, once upon a time a fashionable holiday spot, and still a good place to take the sea air and let the children play on the sand.

• **Get out of town.** Beyond the beach, the coast road follows a lovely shoreline of beaches, cliffs and fishing villages. If you'd rather head inland, just east from Nausicaa there are attractive woods and farmland.

• **Enjoy your lunch.** Boulogne and the surrounding villages have many high-quality restaurants at modest prices. Fresh fish, and especially shellfish, are local specialities.

Boulogne in Three Days

• **Relax in place Dalton.** This big square beside the town's principal church is surrounded with pleasant bars and brasseries. On Wednesday and Saturday mornings it's busy with scores of bright market stalls selling local goods.

Markets are held at place Dalton twice a week

• **Explore the Ville Haute.** The Upper Town is a haven of quiet cobbled streets and squares lined with restored houses. There is much to see, including the domed Basilica.

• **Walk the ramparts.** The grassy pathway on the top of the Old Quarter ramparts gives wide views and makes an enjoyable outing.

• **Visit Nausicaa.** The huge Sea Life Centre on the northern side of town is one of the biggest and best in the world.

• **Drive the Côte d'Opale (Opal Coast).** Beyond Nausicaa, the minor road towards Calais climbs to follow a pretty coastline of beaches, cliffs and fishing villages. From Cap Gris-Nez, there are impressive views across the Channel.

• **Visit Montreuil.** This attractive old hilltop town, a short drive from Boulogne, is guarded by grassy, walkable ramparts and a fascinating citadel.

• **Drive the Course.** One of the prettiest country roads in the area follows the valley of the winding little River Course from Desvres to Montreuil.

• **Enjoy the seaside.** South of Boulogne beach resorts such as Le Touquet and Hardelot-Plage have wide sands, airy promenades and a classy, old-fashioned atmosphere. They make an enjoyable outing from Boulogne.

• **Shopping galore.** Boulogne's main shopping streets in the Ville Basse (Lower Town) have fine food shops and stylish boutiques. There are big supermarkets in town if you prefer, and Cité de l'Europe (► 20) is under half an hour away.

• **Enjoy a gastronomic meal.** Boulogne, Montreuil, Le Touquet and other nearby towns and villages offer a choice of fine restaurants specialising in freshly caught fish and shellfish.

A cobbled street leads to the church of Notre Dame in Boulogne

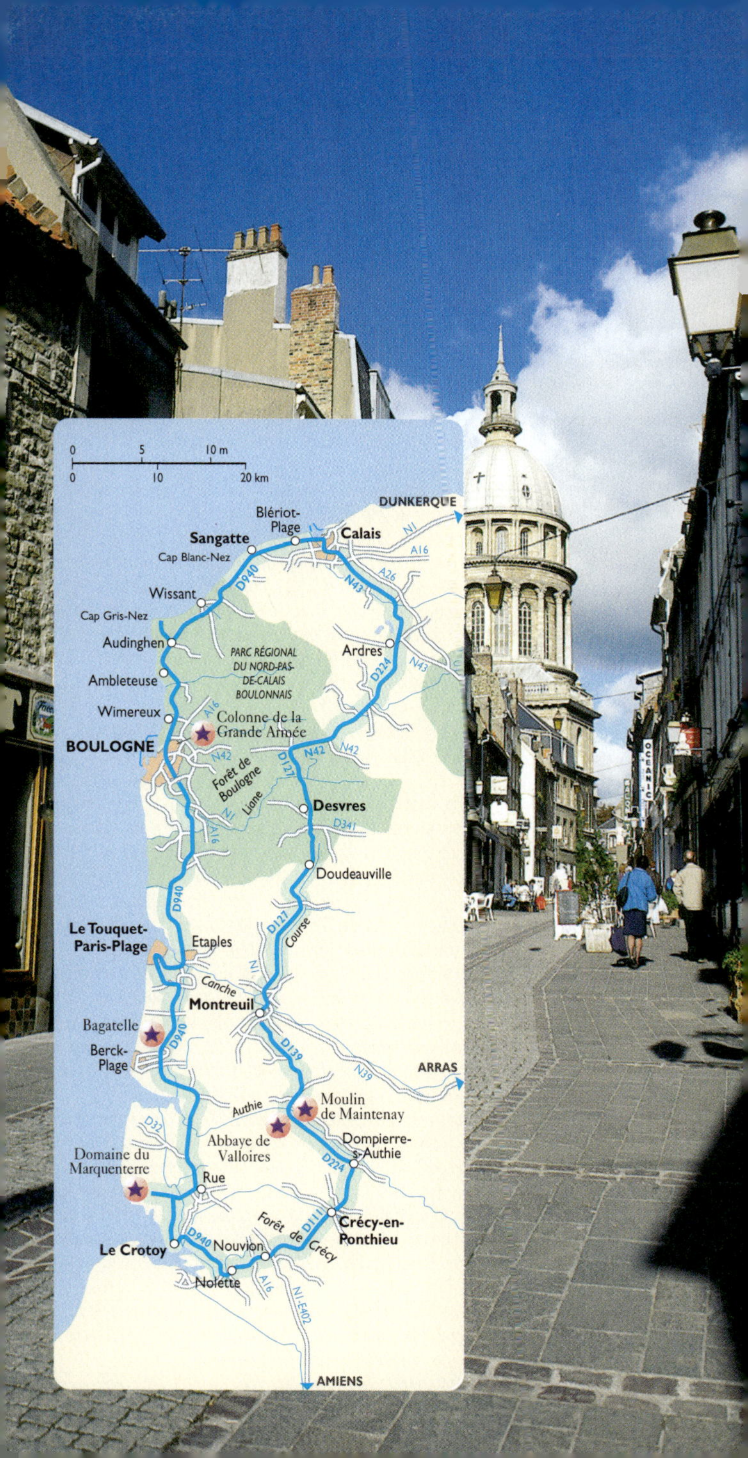

0 5 10 m
0 10 20 km
DUNKERQUE
Blériot-Plage
Calais
Sangatte
Cap Blanc-Nez
Wissant
Cap Gris-Nez
Audinghen
Ardres
PARC RÉGIONAL DU NORD-PAS-DE-CALAIS BOULONNAIS
Ambleteuse
Wimereux
Colonne de la Grande Armée
BOULOGNE
Forêt de Boulogne
Liane
Desvres
Doudeauville
Course
Le Touquet-Paris-Plage
Etaples
Canche
Montreuil
Bagatelle
Berck-Plage
ARRAS
Authie
Moulin de Maintenay
Abbaye de Valloires
Dompierre-s-Authie
Domaine du Marquenterre
Rue
Crécy-en-Ponthieu
Forêt de Crécy
Le Crotoy
Nouvion
Nolette
AMIENS
D940
N1
A16
A26
N43
D224
N42
D127
D341
D139
N39
D32
D111
N1-E402
OCEANIC

A Tour from Boulogne

Distance
272km

Time
72 hours

Start/End Point
Boulogne

Tourist Information Offices
Boulogne
✉ 24 quai Gambetta
Le Touquet
✉ Palais de l'Europe
Montreuil
✉ 21 rue Carnot
Desvres
✉ rue Jean Macé
Calais
✉ boulevard Clémenceau

This tour visits a range of both sophisticated and family-style resorts. The chalk headlands match the white cliffs of Dover, which can be seen on a clear day, glistening in the sun. Behind the coast there are inland river valleys, where quiet villages doze contentedly in the shelter of gently wooded hills.

Boulogne, France's most important fishing port, has a bustling and complex harbour front. Every morning fishermen's stalls offer the freshest possible produce of the sea.

Turn uphill through the busy shopping streets, and you will come to one of the best-preserved historic citadels in the north of France. The castle museum covers a bewildering variety of subjects, including archaeology, ethnology, painting and sculpture, as well as local souvenirs from the time of Napoleon. A pleasant stroll round the towers and fortified gateways of the preserved 13th-century ramparts, which enclose the medieval Haute Ville, gives views of the quays below.

Leave ***Boulogne*** *on the N1, then take the D940 and N39 to* ***Le Touquet-Paris-Plage****.*

Le Touquet grew up in the 19th century, largely as a haven for British gamblers taking advantage of the more lenient French gambling laws. Developed jointly by French and British interests, it has unparalleled facilities for all kinds of sport, including a huge annual motor-sport 'enduro' race on its extensive sands. Three well-kept golf courses occupy the southern outskirts, and the beaches are glorious.

You may think that some of the seafront apartment blocks contrast hideously with the few remaining 19th-century buildings there. The heart of the town, however, retains its elegant shops, cafés and restaurants. Discreet wooded footpaths are threaded through the pine- and birch-woods of the handsome residential suburbs.

Aqualud, on the seafront at Le Touquet, is a modern swimming pool complex. Its water fountains and a 90m curving chute are great fun for children, and adults might enjoy the sauna. On the D940, south of the resort, the fun park at Bagatelle features a roller-coaster ride which finishes with a belly-flop into a lake, a monorail, a mirror maze, roundabouts, an aviary and a zoo.

Leave Le Touquet, following Berck and Hesdin signs, and rejoin the D940 as for Rue. Turn right, following signs to ***Domaine du Marquenterre****.*

Domaine du Marquenterre, a private estate, is one of the finest bird reserves in Europe, created behind a screen of pine trees on land reclaimed from the estuary of the Somme. Residents and migrants include ducks, geese, swans, gulls and waders, hoopoes, avocets, spoonbills, storks and dozens of other species of shore, lake and salt-marsh. Entry is free and you may rent binoculars.

Return from the Domaine and follow signs to ***Le Crotoy.***

Very much a French family resort, Le Crotoy has a good beach, fishing and yacht harbours by the River Somme. Fresh fish and shellfish are available from roadside stalls and in the restaurants. You should take care before imitating the locals' casual-seeming gumbooted strolls across the tidal inlets. Make sure not to be caught by the incoming tide.

The old station is a terminus for the summer railway, whose steam-hauled trains explore the pleasant countryside inland.

Local tourist offices have maps of the network of walks inland from Le Crotoy, in the lovely pastureland behind the Somme estuary. They wander past fields, woodlands and water channels in what was unproductive marshland just a few generations ago.

Leave Le Crotoy by 'Sortie Ville' signs. Turn right on the D940, then left on the D140 to Noyelles. Turn left over a level crossing, then left on the D111 through ***Nolette*** *to* ***Crécy-en-Ponthieu.***

On the exit from Crécy, a viewpoint tower (Le Moulin Edouard III) stands at Edward III's traditional vantage point over the battlefield of Crécy in 1346, when his archers routed the French crossbowmen in one of the most decisive battles of the Hundred Years' War. Edward's son, the Black Prince, who was then little more than a boy, won his spurs here.

Another hero of the Battle of Crécy was the blind King John of Bohemia, brother-in-law of the French king, Philippe VI. A cross marks the spot on the battlefield where he is said to have fallen. According to tradition, this king's emblem was adopted by the Black Prince as the Prince of Wales' Feathers.

At Nolette, between Le Crotoy and Crécy, one of the most unusual cemeteries in France commemorates the 96,000 members of the Chinese Labour Force employed by the Allies during World War I. Its base was near by,

Terrace cafés near the Basilica of Notre Dame in Boulogne

and 870 of the Chinese, who died in an epidemic, are buried here.

Continue on the D111 to ***Dompierre-sur-Authie****, then left on the D224 to* ***Valloires****. After the Abbaye de Valloires turn right to* ***Moulin de Maintenay****, right at a roundabout and left on the D139 to* ***Montreuil****.*

Formerly Montreuil-sur-Mer, the town is now 14km from the sea. It retains many picturesque houses on cobbled and steeply cambered streets; some of the action of Victor Hugo's Les Misérables is set here. A statue of Sir Douglas Haig is a reminder that the British commander-in-chief in World War I made his headquarters near by. Montreuil's historic ramparts provide a beautiful hour-long walk, partly edged with trees and giving splendid sunset views. The abbey church dates back to the 11th century.

Leave Montreuil on the N39, then take the N1 as for Boulogne. Bear right off the N1 for Inxent, then follow the D127 to ***Desvres*** *– a delightful rural route along the Valley of the Course.*

The square at Desvres is the site of regular morning markets, but since the 18th century the main business of the town has been in *faïence* or glazed pottery. Several workshops welcome visitors, and there is a purpose-built pottery museum.

*Leave Desvres on the D127. Turn right on the N42 and then take the D224 to Ardres. In **Ardres** turn left on the N43 and continue to **Calais** (➤ 7–23). Take the D940 from Calais through **Sangatte**, the huge landward base of the French Channel Tunnel, to Cap Blanc-Nez.*

At Sangatte's information centre a comprehensive display explains what massive investment and civil engineering expertise were needed for the opening of the Channel Tunnel.

The road from Calais follows the little farms and high, white cliffs of the Opal Coast, with thrilling views across the Channel to the coast of Kent. West of Calais, there are several smaller fishing ports. One local speciality is *moules* (mussels), often sold from stalls outside the fishermen's homes.

The sweeping chalk headland of Cap Blanc-Nez is introduced by a fine, windswept statue of the pioneer French aviator, Hubert Latham, who was famous, like Blériot, for his 'audacious flights' above the Channel. Turn right for the splendid viewpoint memorial to the French sailors of the World War I Dover Patrol. Turn left for the Musée du Transmanche, devoted to the history of the Channel Tunnel plans, from the earliest hare-brained schemes involving horse-drawn carriages.

The Pas de Calais district played a great part in World War II, and there are several museums about the conflict. Two on the route are at Ambleteuse and in a former German blockhouse at Audinghen.

*Continue on the D940 through **Audinghen**, where the D191, on the right, leads to Cap Gris-Nez.*

The chalk cliffs around Cap Blanc-Nez and Cap Gris-Nez are a nesting ground for gulls and fulmars, which skim the waves and soar on the up-currents of air. Kestrels also nest here, and you may be lucky enough to see one hovering over the grassy cliff-tops before plunging on its prey. The clifftop flora is outstanding during the summer months.

Beyond Wimereux the left turn signed 'vers A16' leads towards the Colonne de la Grande Armée, a towering monument topped by a statue of Napoleon in characteristic pose. He assembled his army here in 1803 for an invasion of Britain which never took place.

*The D940 continues to **Boulogne**.*

What to See

10km north of Boulogne

Museum of World War II
2 rue des Garennes
03 21 87 33 01
Apr to mid-Oct, 9:30–6, rest of year weekends only 10–6
Moderate

Many brasseries and restaurants
Nausicaa
boulevard Ste-Beuve, beside Boulogne beach
03 21 30 99 89
Sep–Jun 9:30–6:30; Jul, Aug 9:30–8. Closed three weeks in Jan
Good, alternative route through exhibition for wheelchair users
Expensive

Boulogne's old town survived intensive bombing during World War II

AMBLETEUSE

This small Opal Coast resort has a large, fascinating and unique **Museum of World War II**, concerned not only with local events but with the whole course of the war, from the Polish Campaign in 1939 to the Japanese surrender in 1945. Also of interest here is Fort Vauban, a 17th-century seashore defence now housing a local history museum.

BOULOGNE

Château Museum (➤ 37, Walk).

Colonne de la Grande Armée is three kilometres out of town on the N1. This immense monument recalls Napoleon's plans to conquer Britain in 1803; his invasion army assembled here – but dispersed after the Emperor changed his mind.

Nausicaa The exciting national Sea Life Centre is a major regional attraction, with French and Dutch coach parties joining British visitors to explore its multifaceted watery displays. Constantly upgrading, it has 27 aquariums and 1.5 million litres of constantly circulating water. The jellyfish tank is one of the most unusual features, and at an open-topped tank you can lean in and stroke the fish. There are sections on human life on the sea, too, such as the trawler out in a storm. It's both educational and entertaining, and has a strongly ecological slant. Nausicaa takes visitors through the whole underwater food chain, from plankton to sharks, with sight, sound and touch. As for taste – the centre has two fish restaurants.

The domed Basilica of Notre Dame stands in the Ville Haute, and is the town centre's principal landmark (➤ 37, Walk).

Boulogne's walled Upper Town or Ville Haute stands on the site of the Roman settlement. Incredibly, though more than 400 bombs were dropped on Boulogne during World War II, not one of them struck the old town. The ramparts date from the 13th century (➤ 37, Walk).

CÔTE D'OPALE (OPAL COAST)

The bright, airy coast road from Boulogne to Calais passes over cliffs, beside rustic farms and through fishing villages. Pause at Cap Gris-Nez and Cap Blanc-Nez for wide, high views across the Channel.

CRÉCY-EN-PONTHIEU (➤ 31, TOUR)

The great battlefield of Crécy, where in August 1346 the forces of England and France clashed, is just a field of cabbages and winter wheat today. In one of the first and

This tile panel is evidence of Desvres' long association with ceramics

bloodiest clashes of the Hundred Years' War, Edward III's 20,000 British soldiers met 60,000 Frenchmen under Philippe VI, and won a resounding victory, thanks to three things the French had not encountered before: disciplined troops, skilled archers and cannon.

LE CROTOY (➤ 31, TOUR)

DESVRES (➤ 32, TOUR)

Ceramics and pottery have been produced in Desvres for over 2,000 years, and this pleasant country town near Boulogne is still a centre for handcrafted and painted fine pottery. Most of the Desvres potteries are open to visitors and have shops in the town's pretty main square. See the story of Desvres pottery in the remarkable and important **Maison de le Faïence**, a building which is itself a wonderful piece of ceramic artwork.

See Tour map
Bars in main square area

Maison de la Faïence
rue Jean Macé
03 21 83 23 23
Apr–Oct Tue–Sun 10–1, 2–6:30; Nov–Mar PM only
Good
Moderate

ETAPLES

Once fashionable with artists, this fishing harbour next to Le Touquet is still very pretty. Today it's noted for fine seafood, displayed in large tanks in shops along the quayside. The Commonwealth War Cemetery here is one of the largest burial grounds in Europe.

3km east of Le Touquet
There are eating places in town but for more choice and high-quality food head into Le Touquet

FORÊT DE BOULOGNE

East of Boulogne, an attractive woodland area of over 200 hectares is criss-crossed with paths and bridle tracks.

8km east of Boulogne

HARDELOT PLAGE

This neat and tidy old-fashioned resort, once rather grand, lies among woods and dunes. It was a favourite with Charles Dickens, who often came here with his friend Ellen Ternan. Wind-driven go-karts race along the broad, sandy beach.

8km south of Boulogne
Eating places include the resort hotels along Ave François 1

MONTREUIL (➤ 32, TOUR)

See Tour map
Inexpensive bars and brasseries in the Lower Town main square, better eating places in the walled Upper Town

In Roman times this lofty little fortified town was a seaport, but it now lies 15km inland. Its grassy ramparts footway gives views over the countryside. Almost everything in the old Upper Town, with its steep cobbled lanes and timbered houses, was built in the 16th century. This was the setting for Victor Hugo's *Les Misérables,* re-enacted in *son et lumière* each summer. The abbey church of Les Saulves dates from the 11th century, as does the neglected walled Citadel, where Sir Douglas Haig, Commander of British Forces, established his HQ during World War I. In Queen Berthe's Tower he could see the coats of arms of thousands of noblemen killed by the English at the Battle of Agincourt, near by, in 1415.

PARC DE BAGATELLE

11km south of Le Touquet
Various eating places in the Parc
Berck-sur-Mer/Merlimont Plage
03 21 89 09 91
Mid-Apr–end Sep 10–6:30
Limited Expensive

A big, popular amusement park with a funfair, a zoo, waterchutes, a wonderfully confusing mirror maze and lots of other children's entertainments. It sits on the dunes just south of the Canche river estuary. Allow several hours.

ST-OMER (➤ 14, TOUR)

LE TOUQUET (➤ 30, TOUR)

VALLOIRES

14km south of Montreuil
Auberge Coq-en-Pâte is a good restaurant in the village
03 22 29 92 09
The abbey is on the edge of the village
03 22 29 62 33
Mid-Mar to mid-Nov daily 10–5 (May–Sep till 6:30)
Moderate
There is a restaurant at Valloires gardens

South of Montreuil and the River Canche, the more rustic River Authie meanders towards the sea. On its bank, the little village of Argoules is the setting for the dignified Cistercian Abbey of Valloires, with its large, enclosed formal gardens and courtyard. In 1346, after the great battle at nearby Crécy (➤ 31, Tour), many of the bodies of the slaughtered French noblemen were brought here.

The abbey prospered, but during the 1740s and 1750s its ancient buildings suffered a series of unexplained fires. Eventually the monks demolished them, and the abbey was replaced with the present château-like building. Today it is a children's home, but is still open for visits. The interior has excellent baroque decoration.

WIMEREUX

There are several restaurants close to the waterfront, such as the Liègoise at the Hôtel Atlantic (03 21 32 41 01) and Epicure (03 21 83 21 83)

Three miles north of Boulogne, on the Opal Coast, this old resort retains its civilised, well-bred atmosphere. It was from here that Marconi made the first radio link across the Channel. In the local cemetery lies the grave of Colonel John Macrae, poet of World War I and author of the lines:

In Flanders fields the poppies grow
Between the crosses, row on row.

A Walk in the Ville Haute

Follow Grande Rue up the hill from the Lower Town to the walls of the Upper Town. Continue straight on to the gateway Porte des Dunes, on the right, which leads into the walled area.

From the gateway you emerge in the place de la Résistance, around which stand some fine restored buildings. The square adjoins the place Godefroy de Bouillon, dominated by the elegant Town Hall (Hôtel de Ville).

Turn left into rue de Lille to the Basilique Notre-Dame, on the left.

The Basilica is a curious building dating from 1827–66.

Leaving the Basilica, continue along rue de Lille to the Porte de Calais gateway. Just before the gateway, turn right towards the château.

Cross the moat to reach the medieval château which now houses a museum of artwork and ethnographic and historical objects.

Return alongside the ramparts in a clockwise direction, climbing on to them at Porte Gayole. The pathway passes Porte des Degrés, the gateway open only to pedestrians, and continues via the Gayette Tower. Beyond, descend at Porte des Dunes.

Distance
3km

Time
2 hrs

Start Point
Grande Rue

End Point
Porte des Dunes

Lunch
Find unpretentious snacks and meals in rue de Lille and near the Basilica

Buy a joint museum pass for the Château Musée and Nausicaá (► 34)

Basilique Notre-Dame
The present Basilica stands on the site of an older cathedral, whose labyrinthine crypt, with painted pillars, survives; below that, there are even older foundations, including a Roman temple dedicated to Diana.

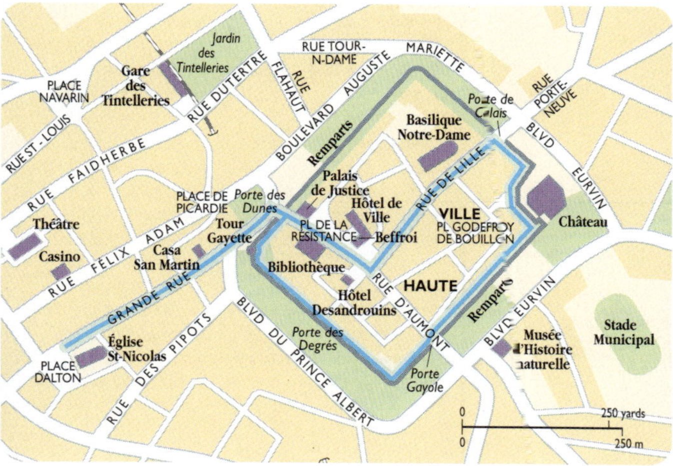

Where to Shop

Gifts and Specialities
An interesting contrast to the fine *chocolatiers* of Boulogne is the home-made chocolate, sold in wonderful, tasty slabs from a signposted house in the village of Beussent, south of Desvres, in the Valley of the Course (no set opening times). Desvres itself, east of Boulogne, has long been famous for producing fine ceramic work. Most of the potteries there have shops in the town's main square.

Boulogne offers bargains, but also quality. Remember that it's not just wine and beer that are less expensive in France, but also perfumes, cheeses and other foods, high-quality kitchenware, baby clothes and – if there's space in the car – garden furniture.

The main streets of Boulogne's Lower Town form a little rectangle, with rue Thiers and rue Victor Hugo on two sides and short sections of Grande Rue and rue Faidherbe along the other two sides. In this compact area the pavements are always crowded with shoppers, and there's an enjoyable, bustling air. You'll find several excellent shops along these streets, where small outlets sell woollen goods, hats, wines, gloves, men's and women's fashions, perfumes, luxurious lingerie, meat, chocolates and coffee.

Boulogne Centre

Canelle Salon de Thé
An excellent place for bread and pastries, where you can also enjoy a coffee.

54 Grande Rue
9–6

La Cave du Fromager
You'll be delighted by the fine cheeses at one of the high-quality shops in the Upper Town. It is attached to a popular restaurant.

23 rue de Lille
Mon, Wed–Sat 9–7, closed 12–2:30

Centre Commercial de la Liane
For quick and convenient shopping, all under one roof, very close to the port. The centre sits on the waterfront boulevard and has a big Champion supermarket as well as many smaller stores.

Corner of boulevard Daunou
Mon–Sat 8:30–8

Le Chais
Sitting alongside Boulogne's main SNCF railway station, this drinks cash-and-carry outlet specialises in the better-quality varieties of French wine.

49 rue des Deux Ponts
Tue–Fri 9–12, 2:30–7, Sat 9–12:30, 2:30–6:30

Fromagerie Olivier
This traditional cheese specialist is among the best-known of all Boulogne's shops. The premises are surprisingly small, but Philippe Olivier sells hundreds of varieties of cheese and supplies many prestigious restaurants. Don't just choose the tried and tested favourites – sample some herby Boulette d'Avesnes, Camembert soaked in Calvados, or super-stinky Maroilles, the original northern cheese (it tastes milder than it smells).

43–5 rue Thiers
Tue– Sat 8:30–12:30, 2:30–7:30

Idriss
This unique shop in the centre of the town sells colourful trays of dried and caramelised exotic fruits. Dates, mangos, figs and lemons are all attractively gift wrapped for you.
24 Grand Rue
Tue–Sat 9–6

Joly Claude
A good *pâtisserie*, with tea rooms attached, in the Upper Town.
44–46 rue de Lille
9–7

Nouvelles Galeries
A department store with quality table and kitchenware at low prices.
57 rue Thiers
Mon 9:15–12, 2–7:15, Tue–Sat 9:15– 9:15 (till 9:30 Fri); closed Sun

Place Dalton
The busy twice-weekly market overflows with stalls loaded with fresh local produce – herbs, flowers, new-laid eggs, live creatures for the pot, quality cheeses, kitchenware and clothes.
Wed and Sat

Quai Gambetta
This morning market is the place to join local house-wives and chefs buying the freshest of fresh fish just off the boats. The hundreds of tons of fish sold here will end up in restaurants all over France. As France's number one fishing port, Boulogne has small quayside stalls selling every kind of seafood, as well as prepared fish pâtés and terrines, stuffed mussels and cockles or dressed crab.
Mon–Sat AM, from 6:30AM

Out of the Centre

Auchan Hypermarket
The biggest and best of the large commercial centres along this main road.
On the N42, direction St-Omer
Mon–Sat 8:30AM–10PM, closed Sun

Les Chocolatde Beussent
At the hamlet of Beussent, a few kilometers from Boulogne on the winding country road that follows the valley of the Course, there's a small traditional chocolate-making business in what is little more than an ordinary house. The little shop sells delicious chocolate treats at modest prices – best of all is chocolate in huge slabs, bought by the kilo. They also have a Boulogne outlet.
At Beussent, on D127 through-road
03 21 92 44 00 (call for opening times)

Cité de l'Europe
The huge shopping complex near Calais is under half an hour from Boulogne on Autoroute A16. (➤ 20)
Coquelles, beside Autoroute A16
Shops: 9AM–10PM, Sat 8:30AM–10PM; closed Sun (except a few shops at the Porte de l'Espagne entrance). Carrefour Hypermarket: Mon–Fri 9AM–11PM, Sat 8:30AM–10PM; closed Sun

Cristal d'Arques
This crystal and glass factory, 50km east of Boulogne at Arques, a suburb of St-Omer, has a showroom, visitor centre and museum, and sells fine glassware at discount prices. Call ahead.
41 & 104 avenue Général-de-Gaulle, Arques
03 21 95 46 47

Leclerc Supermarket
Follow signs for Zone Industrielle de la Liane to reach this large supermarket (or small hypermarket), near the canal and slightly outside the centre of Boulogne. Very popular with locals, it has a good selection of low-priced French foods and other goods, and most of the wines, too, are French.
Centre E Leclerc, Z.I. de la Liane, Outreau
Mon–Sat 8:30AM–8:30PM (Fri till 9PM)

Where to Eat & Drink

Boulogne

La Coquillette (€)

A popular, low-cost eating place with a range of basic dishes.

✉ 10 rue de l'Enseignement-Mutual ☎ 03 21 83 37 51 ⊕ Lunch and dinner. Closed Aug

Chez Jules (€–€€)

A lively brasserie in the marketplace with quick service and good cooking; fish, shellfish, terrines and simpler dishes, including pizzas.

✉ 8 place Dalton ☎ 03 21 31 54 12 ⊕ All day

Le Doyen (€–€€)

A good, friendly little sea-food restaurant near the marketplace.

✉ 11 rue Doyen ☎ 03 21 30 13 08 ⊕ Closed Wed PM, Sun

La Matelote (€€)

Long-established, good-quality fish restaurant in a characteristic hotel, coincidentally nearly opposite Nausicaa.

✉ 80 boulevard Ste-Beuve ☎ 03 21 30 17 97 ⊕ Closed 24 Dec–10 Jan, and Sun PM except Jul–Aug and festivals

Nausicaa (Restaurant de Nausicaa) (€€)

Not the usual 'theme park' mass catering. This excellent fish restaurant is one of the best in town, and provides great value for money.

✉ boulevard Ste-Beuve ☎ 03 21 33 24 24 ⊕ Lunch only

La Poivrière (€–€€)

You may have to wait to be seated at this popular spot in the old town, but the food is of high quality and service is good. The set menus are very good value.

✉ 15 r Lille ☎ 03 21 80 18 18 ⊕ Lunch and dinner

Welsh Pub (€€)

A well-known landmark, with a range of hearty dishes including Welsh Rarebit.

✉ 28 place Dalton ☎ 03 21 31 51 31 ⊕ Lunch and dinner

Inxent

Auberge d'Inxent (€–€€)

A lovely place to linger over a good meal. This delightful, pretty old country inn in a quiet hamlet looks across its garden over the road and down to the gentle valley of the River Course.

✉ On the D127 at Inxent ☎ 03 21 90 71 19 ⊕ Closed 5–31 Jan, Tue PM, Wed exc Jul–Aug

Marquise

Le Grand Cerf (€€)

Attractive old coaching inn, offering good, imaginative dishes, especially fresh fish and shellfish.

✉ 38 avenue Ferber ☎ 03 21 87 55 05 ⊕ Closed Sun PM and Mon

Montreuil

Auberge de la Grenouillère (€€€)

At the bottom of the hill, beside a lazy bend in the river; a wonderful setting in which to sit back and enjoy imaginative, expert cooking.

✉ La Madeleine sous Montreuil, about 3km west on the D917 and D139 ☎ 03 21 06 07 22 ⊕ Closed Jan, Tue and Wed, except. Jul–Aug

Les Hauts de Montreuil (€€)

A low, timbered building dating from 1537 houses this warm, characterful dining room dominated by its large open brick fire-place. Fine cooking with good wines and cheeses.

✉ 21–3 rue Pierre Ledent ☎ 03 21 81 95 92 ⊕ Dinner only

Restaurant Darnetal (€€)

In the shady little square near historic Les Saulves church, at the top of the old heart of Montreuil, this comfortable bar and restaurant is friendly and unpretentious, with modestly priced menus.

✉ 1 place Poissonnerie ☎ 03 21 06 04 87 ⊕ Closed 24 Jun–9 Jul, 20–9 Dec, Mon PM, Tue

Pont-de-Briques

Hostellerie de la Rivière (€€€)

This pretty place, popular with British visitors, offers superb, serious dining featuring fish and shellfish.

✉ 17 rue Gare ☎ 03 21 32 22 81 ⊕ Closed Sun PM, Mon

Le Touquet

Flavio (€€€)

One of the best restaurants in

this classy resort. It has style and flair, and excellent fish.
avenue Verger 03 21 05 10 22 Closed 6 Jan–12 Feb Mon except Jul and Aug

Wimereux

L'Epicure (€€)
Book ahead here to dine on varied and imaginative dishes.
1 rue Gare 03 21 83 21 83 Closed Sun PM, Wed school hols

La Liègoise (€€)
Once one of Boulogne's favourite restaurants. La Liègoise has moved along the coast to the Hotel Atlantic. Downstairs is the brasserie, and upstairs the dining room is done out as a 1930s luxury liner. Fine seafood cooking.
On the waterfront 03 21 32 41 01 Closed Dec–Feb, Sun PM, Mon out of season

Wimille

Relais de la Brocante (€€€)
Unusual, inventive, rather spicy cooking, with an emphasis on fish. This acclaimed eating-place has a good selection of regional cheeses and sumptuous desserts. One of the best on the Opal Coast.
Beside village church 03 21 83 19 31 Closed 25 Jun–10 Jul, Sun PM, Mon

Where to Stay

Stay out of town if you would like places of character, in town for the convenience of being near the shops. All the hotels listed are within half an hour's drive from Boulogne.

Boulogne

Ibis (€€)
Part of a characterless modern chain, but efficient and good value. There are two of them in town – one beside the canal a few minutes walk from the town centre, and another close to the old town near Nausicaa.
boulevard Diderot
03 21 30 12 40
62 rue Porte Neuve
03 21 31 21 01

Metropole (€€)
A modernised, mid-priced hotel and a long-standing favourite for its breakfast garden and perfect central (but quiet) position on the main shopping street.
51 rue Thiers
03 21 31 54 30

Hesdin l'Abbé

Hôtel Cléry (€€)
Very acceptable prices for comfortable, modern accommodation in a splendid old country manor with immaculate gardens. Ten minutes' drive from Boulogne. Good restaurant.
Château d'Hesdin l'Abbé, rue du Château 03 21 83 19 83

Montreuil

Château de Montreuil (€€€)
Perfectly quiet and peaceful location opposite the Citadel entrance. The place to splash out on rooms in a wonderfully grand mansion with beautiful grounds. The restaurant, too, is exceptional – and pricey.
4 Chaussée Capucins
03 21 81 53 04

Les Hauts de Montreuil (€€)
This fine old 16th-century inn has modern, comfortable rooms (some quite small), amiable service and modest prices. The restaurant is outstanding, and there's a wine bar exclusively for hotel guests, where you can enjoy fine wines by the glass.
21 rue Pierre Ledent
03 21 81 95 92

Le Touquet

Manoir Hôtel (€€€)
This famous luxury hotel facing the golf course (reduced fees for guests) has the delicious charm of a grand old Normandy manor house. Large, well-equipped rooms.
avenue du Golf
03 21 06 28 28

Westminster (€€€)
One of the most elegant survivors of pre-war privilege, but with every modern luxury, perfectly equipped rooms and seriously rich guests (many of them British). The hotel's restaurant, Le Pavillon, is a ravishing leftover of 1930s style and service, with first-class cooking.
5 avenue du Verger
03 21 05 48 48

Dieppe and Le Havre

Getting there

April to October a 2-hour high-speed catamaran service runs from Newhaven to Dieppe with three return crossings daily. There's also a four hour traditional ferry crossing three times daily in season. There are three return ferry crossings daily from Portsmouth to Le Havre. The daytime crossing takes around 5½ hours and the overnight trip about 8 hours.

Arriving

On arrival at Le Havre, follow the signs out of the port area. If driving towards Dieppe, take the faster inland autoroute A29 instead of driving along the coast. If heading into the centre of Le Havre, follow signs to Centre Ville. Even if you are heading further afield, it's worth visiting Dieppe. While ferries no longer dock along Dieppe's town centre quayside, the terminal is only minutes from town. For Hoverspeed foot passengers, there's a shuttle bus to the town centre.

The elegant harbour at Dieppe

Dieppe and Le Havre in Three Days

• **Linger at Dieppe's atmospheric quayside.** Once the passenger ferries sailed right into the harbour here, and stalls sold fish straight from the boats. The ferry terminal has now been moved and the stalls shunted along by a new car park, but this is still a lively area, where yachts are moored, and the quay is lined with seafood restaurants.

• **Explore the little shops** of Dieppe's pedestrianised town centre and, if you're here on a Saturday, potter in the market, where fresh fare from sea and land is enticingly displayed.

• **Climb up to the château** on its hill overlooking the town and beach, for the museum and the best view in Dieppe.

• **Visit the region's best gallery.** Named after the novelist and art critic, Le Havre's Musée des Beaux-Arts André Malraux is an intriguing modern building. Visitors can choose how to view the paintings: chronologically from the 17th to the 20th centuries or beginning with the famous collection of works by Eugène Boudin (1824–98) and Raoul Dufy (1877–1953).

If you have time, visit Rouen to view the clock above rue du Gros Horloge

• **Drive the Côte d'Albâtre (Alabaster Coast)**, pausing on this spectacular route at the attractive resorts of Varengeville, Veules-les-Roses, Yport and Etretat.

• **Cross the Seine** via the soaring, hump-backed Pont de Normandie (Normandy Bridge) to the pretty harbour and artists' haven of Honfleur.

• **Take the ferry back** across the Seine further upstream, on one of the tiny river ferries: a *bac*, or small car ferry, sails to and fro from the little town of Duclair, west of Rouen.

• **Tour inland** to see some of Normandy's picturesque, half-timbered villages such as Gerberoy, Lyons-la-Forêt or Les Andelys, on the Seine.

• **Visit Rouen**, the historic capital of Normandy, and walk along the rue du Gros Horloge, admiring the ornate clock whose tower spans the street, and the restored and brightly painted timber-framed shops (➤ 48, Tour).

• **Meet the Impressionists.** Gaze on the River Seine views which inspired them or visit Monet's riverside home and gardens at Giverny.

A Tour from Dieppe or Le Havre

This tour twists along the coast to attractive resorts, bordering the Forêt de Brotonne and the Marais-Vernier.

*Leave **Dieppe** on the D75 to **Varengeville-sur-Mer**.*

You might be deep in the heart of an English county here, with villas and cottages in discreetly private grounds, wooded and grass-banked lanes, and half-timbered farms. There is a wonderful English-style landscape garden at the Parc Floral des Moutiers, the garden of the house called Bois des Moutiers, created by the architect Sir Edwin Lutyens and landscape gardener Gertrude Jekyll. Up on the farmland plateau, the Manoir d'Ango is a Renaissance manor house with a beautiful dovecote.

The artist Georges Braque, a founder of Cubism, is buried beside Varengeville's parish church, for which he designed one of the stained-glass windows.

*Continue on the D75, then go into St-Aubin and follow signs to **St Valery-en-Caux**, leaving it on the D925. Turn right to **Veulettes-sur-Mer** on the D79, then follow the signs to **Fécamp**.*

A fishing, freight and pleasure port at a dip in the cliffs, Fécamp has a shingle-bank beach and some remarkable places to visit. The Palais Bénédictine is the home of the liqueur of the same name, a distillation, first carried out by monks of the Benedictine order, of 27 aromatic plants and spices whose precise recipe is a very closely guarded secret. A museum in the palace traces the history of Benedictine and displays religious art, furnishings and, in the Gothic hall, a magnificent oak and chestnut ceiling built by Fécamp shipwrights. The early Gothic abbey church, La Trinité, is enormous, its nave one of the longest in France.

*Leave Fécamp on the D940 as for Etretat, then go right on the D211 through Yport and follow the D11 to **Etretat**.*

Nowhere on this coast matches Etretat for location. It lies behind a beach at the foot of a wooded valley. To north and south rise tall, white cliffs with weathered natural arches and a great, isolated needle rock a little way off shore.

Paths climb to the cliffs called Falaise d'Amont, north of town, and to the Falaise d'Aval, to the south. Amont probably has the finest overall view, a seafarers' chapel, and a museum to the aviators Nungesser and Coli, whose

Distance
434km

Time
72 hours

Start/End Points
Dieppe

Tourist Information Offices

Le Havre
✉ 186 blvd Clemenceau
Dieppe
✉ Pont Jehan Ango
Fécamp
✉ rue Alexandre le Grand
Etretat
✉ place Maurice-Guillard
Caudebec-en-Caux
✉ place General de Gaulle
Honfleur
✉ Quai Lepaulmier
Rouen
✉ place de la Cathédrale

Start tour from Le Havre
This tour can also start and finish at Le Havre (➤ 46). Make sure you spend some time in Dieppe – it is one of the highlights of the region and is well worth exploring.

The 51st Highlanders
In June 1940, while most of the British troops in France were being evacuated from Dunkerque, the 51st Highland Division was ordered to pull back to Le Havre. In this sacrificial manoeuvre, which helped to divert 10 German divisions, the Highlanders fought until their ammunition was exhausted, and thousands had to surrender at St-Valéry-en-Caux. A granite memorial on a hillside at St-Valéry commemorates the event, and the town is twinned with Inverness, the Highland capital.

plane was last seen over Etretat before disappearing during the first attempt, in 1927, to fly the Atlantic from east to west. There is also a dramatic memorial to them, with a mosaic tricolour of France.

Leave Etretat on the D940 to ***Le Havre****. You may choose to by-pass Le Havre by leaving Etretat on the D39 (signposted for Criquetot l'Esneval). Follow this country road all the way to Tancarville, on the banks of the Seine at the foot of the great Tancarville bridge. Turn onto the D982 for Caudebec-en-Caux.*

Enclosed by industrial suburbs, the centre of Le Havre – entirely rebuilt in 1944 – is the masterwork of architect Auguste Perret, who believed in the beauty and versatility of concrete. His grand boulevards and squares certainly raise concrete above the merely functional, but it's not to everyone's taste. The main street, avenue Foch, has some of the best shopping on the Channel coast.

A splendid fine arts museum, Musée des Beaux-Arts André-Malraux, shows works by Renoir, Pissarro, Sisley and Dufy, among others. The Musée de l'Ancien Havre illustrates the history of the town.

Leave Le Havre on the N15 as for Rouen. Turn right on to the D28 for ***Caudebec-en-Caux****.*

Just downstream from the Pont de Brotonne suspension bridge, which soars over the Seine, Caudebec is set on the commercial side of the river. The Musée de la Marine de Seine covers the history of river boats and river traffic. The remarkable Church of Notre Dame, in 15th- and 16th-century flamboyant Gothic style, has a lovely fretted roof and a west frontage like lacework in stone, with 300 now heavily weathered figures of saints, prophets, musicians and gentlefolk of the town.

A memorial beside the main road commemorates the Caudebec-built Latham seaplane which was lost in 1928 during a rescue mission in the Arctic. Roald Amundsen, discoverer of the South Pole, was one of the crew.

Leave Caudebec-en-Caux on the D982, then turn left to cross the Pont de Brotonne. Go right on the D65, left on the D40, then bear left to ***La Haye-de-Routot****.*

The fascinating village of La Haye-de-Routot lies in farmland on the edge of the Forêt de Brotonne. La Haye's Four à Pain is a restored 19th-century brick-built bakehouse, run as a working museum. The Musée du Sabotier is a workshop museum devoted to clogs (*sabots*). In early summer, look for the 15m pyramid of wood which, on 16 July, is set alight to create the Feu de St Clair, an old pagan ritual taken over by the Church.

Leave La Haye for Routot. Go left, then right, at Stop signs, then continue through ***Bourneville*** *as for Quillebeuf-sur-Seine. Go left on the D95 to Ste-Opportune and straight on at crossroads, following the 'Réserve de Faune' sign. Hairpin right at the T-junction. Turn left at the 3.5t sign, then left at the T-junction. Follow Honfleur signs uphill to the view indicator.*

Bounded by an amphitheatre of wooded hills, this area, the Marais-Vernier, was once marshland flooded by the Seine. At the beginning of the 17th century, Dutch workers dug channels to drain the southern part of the marsh. They are still recalled in the name of the Digue des Hollandais (the Dutchmen's Dyke), alongside the D103. North of that road, the work was tackled only in 1947.

Now the Marais-Vernier is mostly lush grazing land for Camargue horses and Highland cattle. Pockets of boggy ground remain, and there are central scrubby woodlands. In spring, blossom embellishes the surrounding farmland. La Grande Mare is the lake to which most of the drainage water flows on its way to the Seine.

After the view indicator, go right on the D100 to ***St-Samson****, then left past the church on the D39. Bear right to the give-way sign, then left at the T-junction on the N178. Go first right and follow the signs to* ***Honfleur****.*

Birdland

Where the main route turns sharp right after Ste-Opportune, bear left and after less than a kilometre watch for the 'Reserver de Faune' car park. A steeply stepped viewing tower overlooks the nature reserve around the Grande Mare. You will often see mallards, coots, grebes, teal, pochard and tufted duck on the lake itself or in the reed beds and drainage channels round it. Grey herons and Cetti's warblers are present, but more secretive.

The Devil's Castle
After leaving the N138 for the D3 on the way to Rouen, turn right uphill for the Château de Robert-le-Diable. There was no such person as Robert the Devil, but this is a genuine old stronghold of the Dukes of Normandy. In a curious mixture, the castle features a Viking waxworks display, mini-golf and children's games.

Robert the Devil's castle

Honfleur's lovely old slate-roofed houses overlook the sheltered harbour of the Vieux Bassin. Near by are some splendid survivals like the Grenier à Sel (salt stores) in the rue de la Ville. The work of Honfleur-born artist Eugène Boudin, admired for his ability to 'paint the wind', is featured in the museum which bears his name. Another museum has 12 rooms furnished in traditional Norman style and offers visits to the old town prison. The Musée de la Marine is stocked with memorabilia of the sea.

It was from here, that Samuel de Champlain sailed on eight voyages between 1603 and 1620 to explore Canada and found the city of Quebec.

Leave Honfleur by the rue de la République as for Pont-l'Evêque, then go left as for Tancarville on the D17. Turn right on to the N175, then left on the D534 to ***Cormeilles****. Leave Cormeilles on the D810, continue into* ***Lieurey*** *and follow the D137 to* ***Pont-Authou****. Go right on the D130, then left on the D39 to* ***Le Bec-Hellouin****.*

Many old buildings survive in Le Bec-Hellouin, from the tiny red-tiled wash-house by a stream to the ruins of a once powerful 11th-century abbey. Three of its 'sons' became archbishops of Canterbury – Lanfranc in 1070, Anselm in 1093 and Theobald in 1138.

Continue on the D39, then go left on the N138. At the Stop sign, go straight ahead on the D3 as for Rouen, through Moulineaux. Turn right at traffic lights as for Elbeuf, and right over the level crossing. Go sharp left on the N238 and follow the signs to ***Rouen****.*

At the heart of this large industrial city, historic capital of Normandy, is a beautifully restored Old Quarter of narrow lanes and timbered houses, spires and belfries. Stroll along the traffic-free main shopping street, rue du Gros Horloge (the 'Gros Horloge' is the ornate blue, red and gold clock on a massive Renaissance tower straddling the street). It starts at place du Vieux Marché, where Joan of Arc was burned at the stake on 30 May 1431. A 20m concrete cross marks the spot.

Focal point of the Old Quarter is the magnificent Gothic Cathedral of Notre Dame, painted many times by Claude Monet. Additions to the building over the years include the distinctive metal spire, added in the 19th century. Opposite, the Rouen tourist office is housed in a handsome Renaissance former tax office.

Road Races
Roadside barriers along the D132 and N238, a grandstand and a starting grid are part of the Rouen-les-Essarts motor-racing circuit. Fangio was the French Grand Prix winner here in 1957, and the American Dan Gurney won in 1962 and 1964.

Leave Rouen on the N28, then go left on the D928, left on the D151 to ***Bellencombre*** *and left again on the D154 to* ***Dieppe****.*

What to See

ABBAYE DE JUMIÈGES ✪

For centuries this big, rambling and beautiful 11th-century abbey remained one of Europe's grandest, most prosperous centres of religious learning. Today, riverside Jumièges survives as a majestic and evocative ruin.

10km northeast of Routot
02 35 37 24 02 (telephone for opening times)

LES ANDELYS AND CHÂTEAU GAILLARD ✪✪

Clinging to the north bank of the River Seine, delightful Petit Andelys is overlooked by Richard the Lionheart's imposing white hilltop fortress Château Gaillard ('bold castle'), which gives thrilling views along the meandering valley. Grand Andelys, near by, is a pleasant, bustling little country town.

32km southeast of Rouen
Choice of restaurants (€–€€€)

CÔTE D'ALABÂTRE (ALABASTER COAST) ✪✪✪

Alabaster is pure white, and the name refers to the magnificent white-chalk cliffs layered with flint, in places sea-carved into fantastic shapes, which rise above the pretty resorts, bays and beaches along the coast between Dieppe and Etretat (➤ 45, Tour).

Wide choice of restaurants in coastal resort (€–€€)

Beach scenery at Etretat

DIEPPE ✪✪✪

Château-Musée The 15th-century castle which guards the town now houses a museum with Impressionist paintings, displays on shipping and a fascinating collection of beautiful carved ivory pieces made by local craftsmen and sailors working in Dieppe's important ivory trade.

Cité de la Mer, a family favourite by the port, has aquariums and fascinating exhibitions on both the natural and human world of the sea.

See Tour map

Château-Musée
Rue Chastes
02 35 84 19 76
Daily 10–12, 2–6; closed Tue out of season
None   Cheap

Cité de la Mer
37 rue de l'Asile Thomas
33 2 35 06 93 20
Daily 10–12, 2–6

See Tour map
Wide choice of restaurants on quays (€–€€)

FÉCAMP (▶ 45, TOUR) ✪

At the grand old Palais Bénédictine you can discover the origins of the famous liqueur and see how it's made. There is also an art gallery and museum.

55km northeast of Rouen

GERBEROY ✪✪

On the border with Picardy, this flowery little village of old stone cottages is one of the prettiest places in Normandy.

35km southeast of Rouen
Les Jardins de Giverny (€€), closed Feb 02 32 21 60 80

Fondation Claude Monet
84 rue Claude Monet
02 32 51 28 21
Apr–Oct Tue–Sun 9:30–6
Good Expensive

GIVERNY ✪✪✪

The perfectly preserved house and flower gardens of Claude Monet (1840–1926), father of Impressionism, are set on the edge of Normandy and give a fascinating glimpse into his life there in the 1880s and '90s. Don't miss the delightful lily pond, which he painted again and again.

HONFLEUR (▶ 48, TOUR)

27km east of Rouen
La Licorne (€€–€€€) 02 32 49 62 02

LYONS-LA-FORÊT ✪✪✪

This picture-book timbered village, with its flower-decked, wooden houses and covered marketplace, stands in the heart of the Forêt de Lyons, a vast area of quiet beech-woods, tranquil hamlets and wonderful walks.

ROUEN (▶ 48, TOUR)

VARENGEVILLE AND MANOIR D'ANGO (▶ 45, TOUR)

Monet's many paintings of the bridge at Giverny have made it an enduring icon

A Walk Around Veules-les-Roses

Veules-les-Roses is on the coast 26km southwest from Dieppe.

Start at the seafront car park and take the path signposted chemin de Randonnée.

This narrow path involves a climb up the cliff edge.

Continue along rue Bellemere, turn left at rue du Marché and down into place des Ecossais. Continue past the Eglise St-Martin and along rue du Manoir, and then across the junction to the town hall. Turn right, then fork to the left, passing Les Puits de la Vaules. Bear left again, along rue du Vieux Château.

This part of the walk leads past the old stone walls which are all that remain of the castle.

Take the next right turn, along chemin des Cressonnières.

From here you can cross the river to see the watercress beds, then retrace your steps back to the sign.

Turn right, returning to rue du Vieux Château.

After going through the ford at L'Abreuvoir, the route takes you across a tiny sandstone footbridge.

Turn left. Cross the main road into rue Champs Elysées.

Here the walk follows the river Veules and passes two watermills.

After the two watermills take a left fork, zigzag back across the river and return to the main road. Turn right into rue du Bouloir, then take the second lane on the right, to follow the river. Turn right at the road, cross the river for a second time and turn left into rue Melingue. Bear right at the next junction, rue Paul Meurice, then left into rue A-Vasquerie.

This road leads to the lovely ruins of Eglise St-Nicolas. From the former cemetery, a flight of steps leads back down to the seafront car park. Some 3000 Allied troops were evacuated from this spot in 1940.

Distance
2.5km

Time
1 hour

Start/End Point
Seafront car park

Lunch
Cafés and bars along the route

Market Forces
It's worth driving out of Le Havre to visit the smaller markets of other towns and villages. Among the regular morning markets are those at Les Andelys (Sat), Etretat (Thu), Fécamp (Sat), Honfleur (Sat), Lyons-la-Forêt (Thu) and Trouville (Wed, Sun).

Where to Eat & Drink

This pâtisserie in Dieppe has a tempting display

Of all the Channel ports, Dieppe has the biggest choice of unpretentious bars and restaurants. Most put the emphasis firmly on fish and shellfish. Early in the morning, the quaysides are busy with stalls selling turbot, sole, brill and shellfish. Over half the scallops eaten in France come from here. Dieppe has given its name to traditional Normandy dishes. *Marmite dieppoise* is a stew of fish and shellfish. *Sole à la dieppoise* has the fish cooked in cider (or, less correctly, wine), with shallots; the sauce is thickened with cream. It's not far to Normandy's great apple and cream country, the Pays d'Auge, across the Seine – so savoury cream sauces, apple pastry, dry cider and fiery Calvados feature on many menus. Another local speciality is Bénédictine, the liqueur made by monks at Fécamp.
For a snack or a drink while shopping in Le Havre, find a café on a corner in place de l'Hôtel de Ville.

Dieppe

Café des Tribunaux (€€)

Grande Rue ends at the Puit Salé, a focal square with several popular bars and brasseries. Among them is this historic inn of great character.

✉ 1 place du Puit Salé
☎ 02 32 14 44 65
🕐 'All day, every day'

Marmite Dieppoise (€–€€)

This much-loved fish restaurant near the port is still arguably the best in town. *Marmite dieppoise* is, of course, one of the restaurant's strong points.

✉ 8 rue St-Jean ☎ 02 35 84 24 26 🕐 Closed 20 Nov–8 Dec, Feb, Thu PM (except in season), Sun PM, Mon (except public hols)

La Musardière (€€)

On the lively, historic quayside facing the yacht harbour, an excellent fish restaurant perfect for sampling Dieppoise cooking at its best for very modest prices.

✉ 61 quai Henri IV
☎ 02 35 82 94 14
🕐 Closed Mon, except Jul–Aug

Le St-Jacques (€)

Crêperie serving light lunch treats.

✉ 14 rue de l'Oranger ☎ 02 35 40 29 92 🕐 Closed Thu eve

Le Havre

La Petite Auberge (€€)

Not far from the shopping streets, this little half-timbered house has first-class cooking, specialising in fish dishes.

✉ 32 rue Ste Adresse ☎ 02 35 46 27 32 🕐 Closed Sun PM, Mon

Honfleur

L'Ancrage (€–€€)

Popular restaurant near the old harbour. Tables are set on the terrace in season. Good value for money.

✉ 16 rue Montpensier
☎ 02 31 89 00 70 🕐 Lunch, dinner. Closed Jan, Tue eve, Wed in winter

Have a leisurely lunch in one of Honfleur's terrace cafés

L'Assiette Gourmande (€€)
Delicious escargots and seafood at Gerard Bonnefoy's ever-popular quayside tables.
2 quai Passagers
02 31 89 24 88 Closed Sun eve, Mon (except in Aug)

Auberge du Vieux Clochers (€€€)
Impressive, intimate restaurant specialising in seafood but also serving a wide range of meat dishes.
9 rue de l'Homme de Bois
02 31 89 12 06 Lunch, dinner. Closed Jan, Sun PM, Wed

Lyons-la-Forêt

La Licorne (€€–€€€)
This lovely and colourful old half-timbered building is set right in the heart of the village, near the ancient market hall, and is always popular.
place Bensérade 02 32 49 62 02 Lunch, dinner. Closed mid-Dec to mid-Jan, Sun eve, Mon in winter

Rouen

La Couronne (€€–€€€)
A famous restaurant in a 14th-century Norman building, on the place du Vieux-Marché at the end of rue du Gros Horloge, where there are many good restaurants at a wide range of prices. Here the prices are high, but the food is superb.
31 place du Vieux-Marché
02 35 71 40 90
Lunch, dinner

Les Maraîchers (€–€€)
Cheaper options at this restaurant and bistro on the square. Dishes use seafood and snails and, unusually, there are some interesting vegetarian options.
37 place du Vieux-Marché
02 35 71 57 73
Lunch, dinner

Les Nymphéas (€€€)
A gastronomic haven serving game dishes and wonderful fish dishes, plus desserts with a liberal use of Calvados in an old building with a courtyard, near the place du Vieux-Marché.
9 rue Pie
02 35 89 2[illegible] 69 Closed 26–30 Aug, Sun eve, Mon

Les Petits Parapluies (€€€)
Although this is only a tiny restaurant, it always seems to be packed with lovers of some of the great Normandy specialities.
46 rue Bourg 02 35 88 55 26 Closed Sun, Mon

Veules-les-Roses

Les Galets (€€)
Enjoy top-quality fish dishes in this smart restaurant near the delightfully pretty waterfront village of Veules-les Roses.
3 rue Victor Hugo (by the beach) 02 35 97 61 33
Closed 5 Jan–3 Feb, Wed (except in high season), Tue PM

Where to Shop

Dieppe and its region are worlds away from the 'booze run' cash and carry shopping of Boulogne and Calais. Here, whether it's for souvenirs and luxury items like antiques or jewellery, or for fashions, or for high-quality food and wine, you'll join locals at little town shops, stalls and – if you're in Dieppe on a Saturday – one of the best street markets in northern France.
Le Havre is a good town for shopping. The main street, avenue Foch, has some chic, upmarket stores. Rue de Paris, leading south from place de l'Hôtel de Ville, is another smart shopping street, as is avenue Réné Coty, north of the square. There's a street market in avenue Coty every Monday, Wednesday and Friday.

Dieppe Centre

Au St Antoine

Popular with the locals this fine *charcuterie* has a tempting display of goods.

✉ 111 Grande Rue

☎ 02 35 84 25 83

Chocolaterie Roussel

Mouthwatering displays of chocolate and sweetmeats.

✉ 115 Grande Rue

☎ 02 35 84 22 75

Divine

Exquisite silk lingerie. Similar products are sold at nearby Soie Caline.

✉ 23 rue St-Jacques

☎ 02 35 40 11 15

Epicerie Olivier

Round the corner from Grande Rue: a wonderful cheese shop set up by Claude Olivier, father of Philippe Olivier, who runs the cheese shop in Boulogne (► 38).

✉ 16 rue St-Jacques

☎ 02 35 84 22 55

Harvard

One of Dieppe's fashion shops selling stylish mens' clothes. Many other mens' and women's clothes shops can be found on the pedestrianised main streets.

✉ 45 Grande Rue

☎ 02 35 82 69 21

Jacadi

It's worth looking out for kid's clothes in France; this shop sells attractive and practical examples, at good prices.

✉ 218 Grande Rue

☎ 02 35 84 38 61

Jeff de Bruges

Delicious chocolates and confectionery.

✉ 11 rue de la Barre

☎ 02 35 84 41 40

Peggotty

Fashion for adults on Dieppe's main shopping street.

✉ 44 Grande Rue

☎ 02 35 84 90 06

Place Nationale/Grande Rue

Dieppe's famous Saturday street market also spills along rue St-Jacques and rue St-Jean. Slabs of fresh butter, ripe fruit, vegetables, sausages, pâtés, preserved meats, live rabbits and hens, eggs, cheese, herbs, baked goods and piles of shellfish. Other stalls sell kitchenware, clothes and household goods.

🕒 Weekly, all day Saturday

Sergent Major

An excellent range of children's clothes.

✉ 168 Grande Rue

☎ 02 32 14 02 18

Out of Dieppe

Auchan

A huge hypermarket, with everything under one roof, 10 minutes outside town.

✉ Centre Commercial Belvédère, Avenue des Canadiens – N27 (direction Rouen) ☎ 02 32 90 52 00 🕒 Mon–Sat 8:30am–10pm; closed Sun

Le Havre

Auchan

This vast hypermarket is about 10 minutes' drive from the centre of Le Havre.

✉ Centre Commerciale Grand Cap, just off D147 north of the city centre ☎ 02 35 54 71 71 🕒 Mon–Sat 8:30am–10pm; closed Sun

Aux Porcelaines du Berry

Selling a range of charming tableware from linens to crystal. Excellent for gifts.

✉ 138 rue Maréchal Joffre

☎ 02 35 42 34 58

🕒 Closed Sun

Where to Stay

If you need to stay in Le Havre then choose the area to the west and to the north of the town centre. Ste-Adresse is a resort and residential area near the estuary, yacht harbour and beach. The sea-facing boulevard de Verdun, in Dieppe, is lined with good, traditional, mid-priced hotels, with a few more modern establishments among the grand old buildings. If you want a sea view – at any time of year – you should book well ahead. Accommodation is also available in a number of quiet villages near to both Le Havre and Dieppe.

Dieppe

Aguado (€€)
At the town-centre end of the seafront, this excellent, comfortable and welcoming hotel has very modest prices.
✉ **30 boulevard de Verdun**
☎ **02 35 84 27 00**

Europe (€€)
A bright, light, modern hotel with pleasant, spacious rooms.
✉ **63 boulevard de Verdun**
☎ **02 32 90 19 19**

La Présidence (€€€)
The grandest of the town's hotels, with wonderful sea views. Modern, thoroughly equipped rooms and plenty of facilities on the premises. Good restaurant.
✉ **1 boulevard de Verdun**
☎ **02 35 84 31 31**

Les Andelys

La Chaine d'Or (€€–€€€)
With a lovely waterside setting and river views, the hotel has taken its name from the lucrative toll chain which hung across the Seine here. Decent and comfortable, but the high point is its elegant, top-quality restaurant.
✉ **place St-Saveur**
☎ **02 32 54 00 31**

Le Havre

Hôtel Vent d'Ouest (€€)
A good, very comfortable and individual little hotel midway between Ste-Adresse and the town centre. Rooms are themed as 'mountain', 'countryside' or 'sea'.
✉ **4 rue de Caligny**
☎ **02 35 42 50 69**

Mesnil-Val

Hostellerie de la Vieille Ferme (€€)
North along the coast from Dieppe. Charming old inn of beams and flowers, 200m from Mesnil's little beach. In the cosy restaurant, exquisite local dishes are served.
✉ **23 rue de la Mer**
☎ **02 35 86 72 18**

Rouen

Hôtel de Dieppe (€)
This traditional hotel faces the station and has modern, well-equipped rooms. Its restaurant, Le Quatre Saisons, serves local specialities.
✉ **place Bernard-Tissot**
☎ **02 35 71 96 00**

Vastérival, near Varengeville

La Terrasse (€–€€)
This small, traditional old hotel, 15km from Dieppe, has magnificent sea views, clifftop gardens and tennis courts, and an excellent restaurant specialising in sea fare. Very reasonable prices.
✉ **Vastérival** ☎ **02 35 85 12 54**

Bread-making as art

BELLE & BIEN

Cherbourg

Getting there

It is possible to travel by day or, on a longer crossing, by night. Choose between Portsmouth–Cherbourg (3–4 crossings daily; 2 hours and 45 minutes by day, 7–8 hours by night), and Poole–Cherbourg (1 or 2 crossings daily, 4 hours and 15 minutes by day, 5 hours and 45 minutes by night).

Arriving

Ferries dock in the big harbour just east of town. It's a short drive into town, or follow signs for the N13 to leave the Cherbourg area.

A 14-century house in Bayeux

Cherbourg in Three Days

- **Explore the town.** Whether staying in the town or in the surrounding countryside, make time to explore this great seaport and naval base, extensively rebuilt after World War II damage. There's a fresh, wholesome atmosphere, and a feeling of closeness to sea and sky. Don't miss its museums, the hilltop Fort du Roule or the pedestrianised Quartier Central, where medieval buildings survive, especially around rue au Blé.
- **Go to market.** Most towns and villages in this part of Normandy have good street markets full of the fresh produce of land and sea. Cherbourg has markets on Tuesday, Thursday, Saturday and Sunday.
- **Tour the Cotentin Peninsula.** The northern tip, on either side of Cherbourg, is rustic and pretty. On the coasts, the old-fashioned fishing villages are a photographer's dream.

Searching for mussels on the beach near Barfleur

- **See the Bayeux Tapestry.** This world-famous tapestry is an essential part of both British and French history. It's colourful and amusing, and tells the story of the Norman Conquest in comic-strip form.
- **Look for lace** in Argentan, Alençon or Bayeux, where elegant high-quality work is an old tradition.
- **Mont-St-Michel,** one of the most dramatic structures in France, is well worth the drive.
- **Settle down** to a leisurely, no-holds-barred Norman lunch or dinner, tucking in to the rich and creamy local specialities.
- **Have a *Trou Normand.*** It's an interval taken half way through a typically huge Norman meal. Sip a Calvados and get your digestion ready for the second half.
- **Eat St-Vaast oysters**, ideally after a walk along the atmospheric St-Vaast quayside. Vegetarians could try the apple tart and lashings of tangy crème fraîche.
- **Learn about the landings.** A trip along the landing beaches, where thousands of Allied troops began the D-Day invasion in June 1944, is both worthwhile and informative.

A Tour from Cherbourg

*Leave **Cherbourg**, staying close to the harbour, and take the D116, the coast road east from town, to **Barfleur**.*

Barfleur, a quiet, appealing little resort and fishing port, was once an important maritime centre. The ship in which William the Conqueror sailed to defeat the English was built here, and in 1194 Richard the Lionheart sailed from the port to become King of England.

*Follow the coast road as far as **St-Vaast-la-Hougue**.*

Famous for its oysters, St-Vaast is a delightful fishing town with a bustling quayside. The town is named after a Viking 'saint' (not actually canonised); *hougue* is the Viking word for a walled harbour. Ile de Tatihou, the Vauban fortified island in the harbour, hosts a summer music festival.

*Take the D902 to **Valognes**.*

In its 17th- to 19th-century heyday, Valognes was 'the Versailles of Normandy', where aristocratic families had their town houses. The bombardments of 1944 wrecked the centre, which has been rebuilt, and also destroyed part of the Church of St Malo. Now a modern concrete nave and tower stand beside the 14th-century chancel.

However, several of Valogne's mansions survived. The elegant 18th-century Hôtel de Beaumont is open to visitors. The Hôtel de Thieuville houses the Musée de l'Eau de Vie et des Vieux Métiers, whose two main subjects are brandy and leatherwork. The Musée du Cidre concentrates on apples and cider-making.

*Take the busy N13 past **Carentan**, across the Cotentin Marshes and beyond **Isigny-sur-Mer** (famous for its butter and cream), and turn on to the D514 for **Grandcamp-Maisy**, on the Landing Beaches Coast.*

Most side roads to the left of the D514 here reach memorials and, beyond, the Americans' principal D-Day landing beach, although signs for Plage d'Omaha lead to a holiday camp. Look for Wn62, a high-set German strongpoint above the shoreline with American monuments and explanations of the D-Day action and German defences. The American cemetery for the men lost during the landings is close by, and there is an exhibition in a prefabricated wartime building at the village of Vierville.

*Follow the D514 and the D6 into **Bayeux**.*

Distance
456km

Time
12 hours

Start/End Point
Cherbourg

Tourist Information Offices
Cherbourg
✉ quai Alexandre-III
Barfleur
✉ Rond-point Guillaume-le-Conquérant
Valognes
✉ place du Château
Bayeux
✉ Pont St-Jean
Arromanches
✉ rue du Maréchal Joffre
Clécy
✉ place du Tripot
Bagnoles-de-l'Orne
✉ place du Marché
Villedieu-les-Poêles
✉ place des Costils
Barneville-Carteret
✉ place Flandre-Dunkerque, Carteret;
✉ 10 rue des Ecoles, Barneville

The cathedral at Bayeux has wonderful stained-glass windows

Most of the fine historic buildings in Bayeux survived the 1944 campaign. You can stroll through old streets and over narrow bridges, admiring the gleaming stonework of the mills on the River Aure. On the ring road, the Musée de la Bataille de Normandie is 'guarded' by British, American and German tanks. Everything in Bayeux, however, pales in importance beside the priceless 11th-century tapestry, with its lively scenes of the Norman Conquest of England, displayed in the Centre Guillaume le Conquérant.

Alongside the cathedral, the Musée Baron Gérard shows paintings, lacework and ceramics.

Leave Bayeux on the D516 and head for ***Arromanches-les-Bains****.*

Without massive supplies, the D-Day landings could not have developed into an advance across the whole of France. Arromanches was the scene of one of the greatest engineering feats of the war – the building, from thousands of tons of prefabricated parts shipped across the Channel, of Port Winston, the giant Mulberry (artificial) harbour. It threw a 5.7km breakwater round the sea approaches to

Arromanches, from which pontoon bridges reached to the shore, and was operational within 12 days.

Today, Arromanches is a busy but unremarkable little resort on a bay between all but vertical cliffs. A viewpoint on the eastern cliff overlooks the many sections of the artificial harbour which remain offshore. On the seafront, the Musée du Débarquement illustrates the creation and operation of 'the key to the liberation of France'.

A tank stands outside the Musée du Débarquement on the seafront at Arromanches

Continue on the D514 to ***Courseulles-sur-Mer****. Here, turn inland on the D79 to the D35 and turn left. Follow this country lane to the River Orne, crossing the river on* ***Pegasus Bridge****.*

In the eastern sector of the D-Day landings, the years of planning and training came down to one audacious feat. Just after midnight on 6 June 1944, three gliders with no room for a conventional approach crash-landed beside this little tilting bridge on the Caen–Ouistreham canal. British troops poured out and after four minutes' fierce fighting secured the bridge. They held it until reinforcements arrived, most decisively the Commandos led by Lord Lovat, who had fought their way inland from Sword Beach. Three columns in the scrubland southeast of the bridge show where the gliders landed. On the west side, a museum tells the story of that dramatic engagement. In November 1993 the original Pegasus Bridge was replaced by a wider, stronger bridge.

Drive towards ***Caen****, taking the ring road round to the D562 turning, signposted Domfront. Turn left on the D132 to* ***Bretteville*** *and the D23, for a winding route following the Routes des Crêtes through the scenic Suisse Normande region. Turn on to the D133c for* ***Clécy****.*

The River Orne at Clécy makes a dramatic curve below the densely wooded cliffs of La Suisse Normande (Norman Switzerland). Don't expect a Swiss-like landscape of lakes and mountains, though this is one of the most beautiful parts of inland Normandy. In Clécy's pleasant town centre, with its 18th-century houses, look for the Musée Hardy, which displays the work of a local artist. An exhilarating walk climbs to the magnificent viewpoint of the Pain du

Pointe du Hoc

Turn right off the D514 after Omaha Beach for Pointe du Hoc. Here a viewpoint and memorial at the remains of a clifftop German observation point look out over the sheer rocks scaled by 225 US Rangers during the D-Day landings. The **Musée des Rangers** at Grandcamp-Maisy, 5km away, traces the history of the Rangers and their astounding achievement (30 quai Crampon 02 31 92 33 51 Easter–Sep daily 10.30–6; rest of year by appointment only).

Moving Dunes
Until early this century, the huge sand dunes north of the Cap de Carteret were moved steadily inland by the wind, engulfing roads and a mill. You can see how, classified as a nature reserve, they have now been stabilised with the planting of marram grass thickets. Look for birds such as Dartford warblers and stonechats, as well as numerous lizards.

Above: *one of the beaches at Barneville-Carteret*

Right: *signposts at Granville*

Cliff Walk
At Barneville-Carteret, an exhilarating walk known as the Sentier des Douaniers (Excisemen's Path) starts from either of the beaches flanking the Cap de Carteret. It follows the contours of the lichen-clad cliffs and passes the site of an 18th-century coastal gun battery.

Sucre (the Sugarloaf), overlooking the Orne. The 16th-century Manoir de Placy houses the Musée des Antiquités Normandes, with a miniature railway and a train museum in the grounds.

From Clécy, take the D562 (which becomes the D962) towards Flers, turning left on to the D924 before the town. Follow this as far as the D53, on the right, which leads to ***Bagnoles-de-l'Orne****.*

Retaining its old prominence as the most popular spa town in the west of France, Bagnoles, with the linked Tessé la Madeleine, lies among woodlands rising from the banks of La Vée river. People come here for bath cures and 'to take the waters', but Bagnoles also offers excellent sporting facilities: golf, tennis, swimming, horse-riding, fishing and archery. Bagnoles' casino backs on to a very pleasant lake, where pedaloes can be hired.

Leave Bagnoles on the D335, joining the D908 for Domfront. Go through ***Domfront*** *town centre and continue on the D907 to* ***Mortain****. Pick up the D33 for* ***Villedieu-les-Poêles****.*

If every place name tells a story, how to explain Villedieu-les-Poêles – 'God's Town of the Pots and Frying-Pans'? The Knights of Malta (a military religious order), established here in the 16th century, called the place Villedieu, and it became a famous centre of craftsmen and metalworkers.

That great tradition continues. You can watch hand-beaten copper being worked at the Atelier du Cuivre and pewterware at the Maison de l'Etain. The Fonderie des Cloches is a bell-foundry open to visitors, and the Maison de la Dentellerie displays the lacework for which the women of the town were known all over northern France.

Take the D924 to ***Granville****.*

Like Monaco, Granville expanded from a fortified town on a promontory rock. Originally, thanks to the contortions of history, it was

The town of Clécy is the centre of the Suisse Normande region

fortified by the English against the French. The story of the town is illustrated in the Musée du Vieux Granville, just inside the drawbridge gateway of the Haute Ville (High Town).

The 15th-century Notre Dame Church stands among the alleyways of the High Town, and a good aquarium here includes shell and mineral collections.

On no account miss Granville's Jardin Public. Its lush lawns, pine trees and beautifully laid-out flower beds surround the pink-and-white villa once owned by couturier Christian Dior.

Ferries sail from Granville to La Grande Ile, with its château built by motor magnate Louis Renault.

*Take the D971 to **Bréhal**, and turn left on to the D20. Turn on to the D650. On meeting the D903, follow it round towards **Barneville-Carteret**.*

The two little towns of Barneville and Carteret, administratively linked, form a family holiday resort with excellent sands, a rocky headland and a sheltered tidal river harbour. This is a pleasant walking and watersports area, and summer ferries sail to the Channel Islands. Make for the lighthouse on Cap de Carteret, a wonderful viewpoint. Take care at any family bathing parties. While the town beaches have a lifeguard service, the quieter one north of the Cap does not. There, it is all too easy for youngsters to be taken well out of their depth.

*Leave Barneville for Bricquebec on the D902. At airy **Bricquebec**, with its ruined medieval fortress, turn on to the D900 for the journey back into **Cherbourg**.*

Ste-Mère-Eglise

This was the first French town liberated on D-Day. A parachute-shaped museum describes the landings by the 82nd US Airborne Division, and tells the tale of Private John Steel, whose parachute caught on the church steeple. He dangled from the roof for two hours before being rescued, and the event is commemorated with the model of a paratrooper, hung from the steeple every summer.

What to See

24km southeast of Bayeux
Restaurants, cafés and bars (€–€€€)

Le Mémorial de Caen – Musée pour la Paix
esplanade du Général Eisenhower
02 31 06 06 44
Feb–Nov daily 9–7 (till 8 mid-Jul–end Aug); rest of year till 9–6
Good
Expensive

Restaurants on quai de Caligny (€–€€)

Cité de la Mer
Gare Maritime Transatlanique
08 25 33 50 50
Jun–mid-Sep daily 9–7; mid-Sep–May 10–6
Good; no access to submarine section
Expensive

Musée de la Guerre et la Libération
Fort du Roule
02 33 20 14 12
May–Sep daily 10–12, 2–6 (closed Sun, Mon AM); Oct–Apr Wed–Sun 2–6
Good
Cheap

Top right: *the dramatic outline of Mont-St-Michel*

Bottom left: *the marina at Port Chantereyne*

BARNEVILLE-CARTERET (➤ 63, TOUR)

BAYEUX (➤ 59–60, TOUR)

CAEN ✪✪✪

Entirely rebuilt after World War II, Caen is a city of parks and trees. Its historic centre clusters beside William the Conqueror's castle, which contains a Musée des Beaux-Arts (Fine Arts Museum). The Conqueror also built the Abbaye aux Hommes (Men's Abbey) and the Abbaye aux Dames (Women's Abbey) for his wife, Mathilde. On the edge of the city, **Le Mémorial de Caen – Musée pour la Paix** (Peace Memorial), a permanent exhibition on war, is one of Caen's most interesting sights. Multimedia presentations deal with the 1944 Battle of Normandy and the world's failure to keep peace since 1945. Other rewarding museums include Musée-Pégasus (about 1944 Liberation), Musée de Normandie, Musée de la Poste, Musée de la Nature, and the fascinating Plan de Rome, a scale model of 1st-century Rome at the University of Caen.

CHERBOURG ✪✪

The extensive **Cité de la Mer**, a scientific and educational museum located in the former transatlantic port, mainly deals with man's relationship with the sea both on the surface and in the depths.The hilltop stronghold of Fort du Roule commands an immense view of harbour, town and sea, and houses the interesting **Musée de la Guerre et la Libération** (Museum of the War and Liberation), tracing the history of World War II with original maps, plans, scale models and photos. The Musée Thomas-Henry is Cherbourg's Fine Arts Museum, with a wide range of artworks from the 15th–19th centuries, including a collection of some 30 works by Millet. The **Museum Liais**,

in a park, is an ethnographic museum with a wide range of exhibits on various subjects, including a section devoted to the Inuit people of North America.

Port Chantereyne, the marina near the centre of town, is the busiest yacht harbour in France (about 10,000 arrivals annually), thanks partly to its popularity with Channel Islanders. It has its own museum devoted to the wartime role of the Merchant Marine.

Museum Liais
- parc E Liais
- 02 33 53 51 61
- May–Sep daily 10–12, 2–6 (closed Sun, Mon AM); Oct–Apr Wed–Sun 2–6
- None
- Cheap

LA HAGUE ✪

Picturesque bays indent the shoreline of this peninsula west of Cherbourg, while the interior is criss-crossed with 360km of footpaths and bridleways. To the south Europe's highest sea cliffs (128m) give exhilarating views.

- Le Moulin à Vent (€), at St-Germain des Vaux, is a pleasant eating place in a small village

LANDING BEACHES ✪✪✪

The D514 from Grandcamp-Maisie to Ouistreham follows the Normandy beaches where thousands lost their lives in the Allies' surprise invasion in June 1944.

MONT-ST-MICHEL ✪✪✪

Reached across a long causeway, this awesome pyramid-like rock rises from a vast area of wet sands. The stupendous abbey church at the summit has been a place of pilgrimage since the Middle Ages. The picturebook setting and perfect visual harmony have made this one of the most popular sites in France.

Mont-St-Michel
- 23km south of Granville
- Restaurants and cafés (€–€€€)

A Walk Around Barfleur

Distance
3.25km

Time
1 hour

Start/End Point
rue St-Thomas-Becket

Lunch
Quayside cafés, terraces and seafood stalls

Essential maintenance at low-tide at Barfleur

Barfleur is on the coast 30km east of Cherbourg.

This route takes you past the granite buildings and busy port of Barfleur, famous for its seafaring history and its delicious *fruits de mer* (shellfish).

Start at the harbour end of the main road, rue St-Thomas-Bècket, and walk along the quai Henri Chardon.

After passing the Eglise St-Nicolas, the quay leads to the Station de Sauvetage (Lifeboat Museum) at the end. This stretch of coast is often treacherous, and is well known for its swift currents; Barfleur boasts France's first lifeboat station and one of its tallest lighthouses.

Take the narrow alleyway, just before the museum, to the place de l'Eglise. Turn right into rue St-Nicolas.

On the route back to the quay are the house of late artist Paul Signac and potters' studios and antiques shops.

Turn right up the main road, take the second turning on the left and cross place Général de Gaulle into rue Pierre Salley.

After passing an unusual chimney-lighthouse, the walk leads across the bridge and past the Communauté de la Bretonne nunnery (on the right). Take the next left along rue du 24 Juin on to the jetty for good views of the village.

Return along a path to the right by the water's edge.

You now pass another (small) lighthouse, the Feu Aval. Many ships have foundered off these shores, the most famous being the Blanche Nef (White Ship), which was wrecked on the rocks in 1120. It was carrying the only son of English king Henry I, plus 300 nobles. The prince escaped in a small boat, but returned to the doomed ship to rescue his sister. On reaching the ship, his tiny boat sank under the weight of the nobles and crew who clambered on board.

Retrace your steps to the bridge. Continue to hug the harbour, following a narrow gravel passage to the right. Rejoin the road opposite a gateway marked Porte Ste-Catherine. Enter through here, cross the 14th-century Cour Ste-Catherine (courtyard) and return to the main road.

Where to Shop

Rue Albert Mahieu, rue du Commerce and the surrounding pedestrianised streets are Cherbourg's main shopping area, where you'll find many small shops offering a wide choice of high-quality foods and wines, farm-made cider, Calvados, cheese, cream and butter, stylish clothes and kitchenware at much lower prices than in the UK, and many other goods.

Cherbourg Centre

Ambiance et Styles

Attractive kitchenware and a wide range of other goods for the home.

✉ 6 rue Dufresnes

☎ 02 33 93 49 92

Carrefour

A hypermarket in the centre of town, with a branch of The Wine and Beer Company, the well-known British-run cash and carry chain, selling a huge range of wines, beers and spirits at rock-bottom prices.

✉ quai de l'Entrepôt ☎ 02 33 23 38 38 ⌚ 8:30AM–9PM; closed Sun

Jeff de Bruges

A branch of the chain selling top-quality chocolates and confectionery.

✉ rue des Portes

☎ 02 33 53 00 20

Lejetté

One of the best of the shops on the oddly named rue Grande Rue (Cherbourg's oldest street), where there are several *épiceries fines* (delicatessens), *charcuteries* and *traiteurs* (specialists in cooked meats, fine cheeses and prepared dishes) with enticing window displays.

✉ 9 rue Grande Rue

☎ 02 33 53 01 37

Manoukian

The place to browse among the latest fashions.

✉ 24 rue du Château

☎ 02 33 93 32 39

Quimerc'h

Another attractive shop selling sausages, pâtés, terrines, hams, savoury pastries, fine Calvados and *cidre bouché*, the dry cider of the region.

✉ 22 rue Grande Rue

☎ 02 33 53 00 70

Salon de Thé Yvard

The best pâtisserie in town – the perfect place not just to buy but to sit and relax over a coffee and a pastry. On Sundays, they have *meringue à la crème chantilly*, which is wonderful.

✉ 5 place de la Fontaine

☎ 02 33 53 04 14

Séduction

A well-named shop selling seductive fine lingerie. Lingerie can also be found at Fine Ligne ✉ 13 rue Christine.

✉ 36 rue du Commerce

☎ 02 33 53 18 72

Vanille

Stylish and attractive children's clothes.

✉ 7 rue François la Vieille

☎ 02 33 53 28 66

Out of the Centre

Auchan

The biggest of the hypermarkets, where you can buy everything conveniently under one roof, sometimes sacrificing a little on quality but gaining in lower prices. It also has bars and a self-service restaurant.

✉ Centre Commercial du Cotentin, at La Glacière, 5km from Cherbourg on N13

⌚ Closed Sun

St-Vaast-la-Hougue

Gosselin

Excellent wines and a surprisingly good range of whiskies in this fine grocers shop on the Saturday market street.

✉ 27 rue Verrue

☎ 02 33 54 40 06

⌚ Closed Sun afternoon, Mon

Market Days

Place Général de Gaulle, the main square, dominated by its exuberant theatre, is filled with colour and atmosphere on Tuesday, Thursday and Saturday, when stallholders set up with an abundance of fruit, vegetables, geese, ducks and hens, shellfish, dairy produce and brilliant flowers.

Where to Eat & Drink

The Cotentin Peninsula, with Cherbourg at its tip, is famous among French gourmets for its lamb *de pré salé* (from saltwater meadows), its *fruits de mer* (shellfish; the west coast supposedly has the best in the world), and its sea fish, its local butter, tangy crème fraîche and cheese, tart apples from the thousands of local orchards and vegetables grown in the region's particularly light but rich soil.
However, restaurants are relatively scarce here because, as locals say, they are so happy at the family table that they have no need to eat out. The one exception is crêperies, or pancake houses. Crêpes are paper-thin pancakes sprinkled with almost anything edible, sweet or savoury, and they are the favourite cheap, traditional fast-food of Normandy.

Bayeux

Le Lion d'Or (€€)
Inside a wonderful hotel of old-fashioned style and charm, here is a warm, welcoming restaurant that somehow combines rustic simplicity with the heights of refinement. Delicious cooking brings together a love of tradition and imaginative flair. Good wine list.
✉ 71 rue St-Jean ☎ 02 31 92 06 90 ⌚ Closed 20 Dec–20 Jan

Caen

La Bourride (€€€)
Gastronomic high spot amongst many decent eateries. This is the place for fresh lobster or *tripes à la mode*, especially out of season in front of a blazing log fire.
✉ 15 rue Vaugueux ☎ 02 31 93 50 76 ⌚ Closed Sun

Carteret

La Marine (€€)
Considered by some to be the region's best eating place, La Marine is right on the quayside, within sight of the fishing boats which bring in most of its produce. Oysters and lobsters are specialities.
✉ 13 rue de Paris ☎ 02 33 53 83 31 ⌚ Closed Mon lunch, Mon eve in Feb, Mar, Oct

Cherbourg

Café de Paris (€–€€)
This big, popular and appealing waterfront restaurant is a Cherbourg institution, and ideal for good-quality fresh fish and seafood.
✉ 40 quai Caligny ☎ 02 33 43 12 36 ⌚ Closed 1–15 Jan

Le Faitout (€€)
Good food in home-cooked style, at reasonable prices, in this convivial, popular town-centre brasserie.
✉ rue de la Tour Carrée
☎ 02 33 04 25 04
⌚ Closed Mon lunch, Sun, two weeks at Christmas

Mont-St-Michel

Mère Poulard (€€€)
If you feel like a snack or a meal while visiting this extraordinary but exhausting site on the watery frontier between Normandy and Brittany, pop into 'Mother Hen's' and sit down to the greatest of Mont-St-Michel's specialities – omelette de la Mère Poulard. If you're in more serious dining mood, this also happens to be one of the Mont's best places for all the classic local dishes.
✉ Grande Rue ☎ 02 33 60 14 01 ⌚ Daily until 9:30PM

St-Germain-des-Vaux

Le Moulin à Vent (€)
Way out on the very tip of the long, narrow La Hague peninsula west of Cherbourg, this pretty, welcoming and good-humoured eating place serves delicious local dishes at modest prices.
✉ In village ☎ 02 33 52 75 20

St-Vaast-la-Hougue

France et Fuschias (€€–€€€)
One of the loveliest little hotels in the area also has one of the most enticing restaurants, filled with a magnificent fuschia that gives a strange inside-outside confusion, and

serving delicious meat, vegetables, fish and seafood at immaculately laid tables. Most of the food comes straight from the quayside or from their own farm.

✉ 18 rue du Marechal Foch
☎ 02 33 54 42 26
🕐 Closed 5 Jan–26 Feb; Mon, Tue lunch in winter

Trelly

La Verte Campagne (€€)
Well down the peninsula, south of Coutances and St-Lô, Trelly is a rustic hideaway which has been put firmly on the gourmet map of France by this tiny, delightful restaurant with rooms. The beams and flowers in this 13th-century farmhouse form the perfect setting for the finest of local dishes, such as lamb *de pré-salé*, game, imaginative fish dishes and, to finish, a spice-bread ice-cream.

✉ Le Hamel au Chevalier
☎ 02 33 47 65 33 🕐 Closed 25 Nov–8 Dec, 15 Jan–8 Feb

Where to Stay

Bayeux

Le Lion d'Or (€€)
Quietly situated (the hotel is a Relais du Silence) but in the heart of town, this historic inn lies back from the road within a handsome paved courtyard. It's thoroughly modernised and has tremendous style and charm, as well as an excellent restaurant.

✉ 71 rue St-Jean
☎ 02 31 92 06 90

Carteret

La Marine (€€)
Dreamily located on the waterfront of a really attractive little fishing harbour, this reasonably priced, family-run hotel has smallish but comfortable rooms facing the sea. A well-placed terrace is ideal for relaxed outdoor eating and drinking, and the hotel's restaurant is one of the best in Normandy.

✉ 13 rue de Paris
☎ 02 33 53 83 31

Cherbourg

Chantereyne (€€)
Facing the busy marina, a rather impersonal but efficient and professional modern hotel, enclosed by a little garden.

✉ port Chantereyne
☎ 02 33 93 02 20

Le Louvre (€€)
This moderately priced, mid-range establishment close to the town centre and the marina has comfortable rooms, 24-hour reception and secure parking.

✉ 28 rue Paix
☎ 02 33 53 02 28

Mercure Hôtel (€€€)
A fine, modern three-star hotel at the harbourside, with spacious, well-equipped rooms and its own decent, moderately priced restaurant. Conveniently located near the town centre.

✉ Gare Maritime
☎ 02 33 44 01 11

St-Vaast-la-Hougue

France et Fuschias (€–€€)
A huge and ancient fuschia clings to the outer walls of this comfortable, civilised, family-run hotel, and even climbs inside the dining room. Rooms are pretty, and look out over a pleasant garden. The hotel's excellent restaurant is a major plus, many of its ingredients coming straight from the working harbour, a few minutes' walk away.

✉ 18 rue du Marechal Foch
☎ 02 33 54 42 26

Valognes

Grand Hôtel du Louvre (€€)
A historic coaching inn with a paved courtyard, this fairly modest two-star establishment has pleasant and well-furnished bedrooms, which are all en-suite, and its own decent restaurant.

✉ 28 rue Religieuses
☎ 02 33 40 00 07

Ostend and Bruges

Getting there

At the moment there is no direct passenger ferry from the UK to Ostend. With fast motorways now linking Calais to Ostend and Bruges, growing numbers of leisure travellers prefer to cross there and make the 110km drive. For foot passengers, operators sometimes provide a Calais-Ostend coach service.

Arriving

If crossings to Ostend resume, the ferry port is just minutes by foot from the town centre. In addition, a major road link exits from the harbour and runs into motorway A10 for Bruges and Brussels.

Frozen canal and windmill near Damme

Ostend in Three Days

- **Explore Ostend.** The pre-war resort has much to see, good town-centre shops, and a pleasant seaside atmosphere.
- **Tour the coast.** Other old-established resorts on the coast deserve a visit, like De Panne. There's a tram which runs the whole length of the Belgian coast several times daily, allowing you to get off at any of the towns on the way.
- **Go to Bruges.** Whether you have come mainly to shop, to sightsee, or to tour, it's vital to spend part of the time in Bruges, one of the most beautiful, best-preserved medieval towns in Europe.
- **Order a beer.** Belgium is the world capital of beer, with over 400 locally brewed varieties, and a staggering range of flavours and qualities. So don't just say 'a beer, please' – if you need help, ask the barman. They're glad to advise.

See a wide range of architectural styles in the Burg at Bruges

A Tour from Ostend

This circular tour begins and ends at Ostend (Oostende), the second busiest port in Belgium, which has grown from a 19th-century royal resort to a small city. It has a yacht-jammed harbour and a busy Fishermen's Wharf, Visserskaai, and behind the seafront are dunes studded with World War II German coastal defence bunkers.

Follow the N34 from ***Ostend*** *(the route of the coast road and coast tram) through the beach resorts to* ***De Panne.***

Strong winds and firm sand have made De Panne, near the French border, an ideal location for sand-yachting, both for competitions and for fun.

Take the N35 for 6km to reach ***Veurne.***

Situated in the polderland, some 6km behind the coast, Veurne (Furnes) was a Spanish garrison town under the Habsburg Empire. Its 17th-century Grote Markt (Main Square) is one of Belgium's most perfect Flemish Renaissance ensembles; a museum in the ornate Stadhuis (Town Hall) features leather wall-hangings from Córdoba and Mechelen. The imposing 13th-century Sint-Walburgakerk (St Walburga's Church) is the focus of the town's renowned Boetprocessie (Procession of the Penitents).

Distance
220km

Time
72 hours

Start/End Point
Ostend

Tourist Information Offices
Oostende (Ostend)
Monacoplein 2
Gent (Ghent)
Crypt of the Belfry Tower, St Baafsplein 17A
Brugge (Bruges)
Burg 11

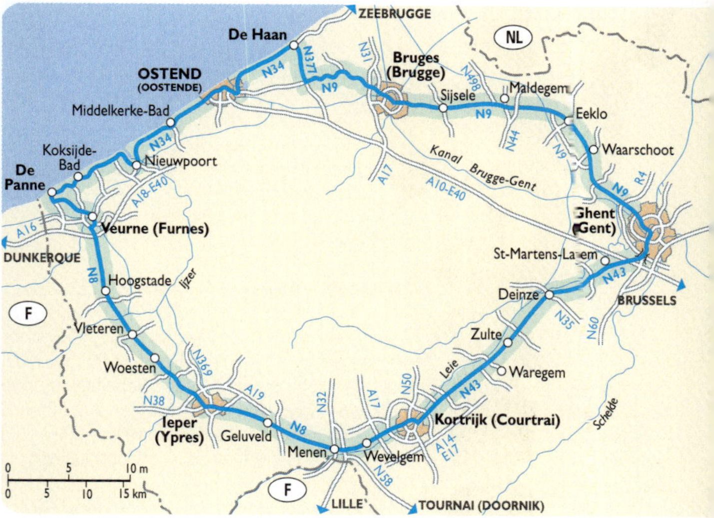

Veurne's Grote Markt is an excellent place to enjoy café life

Take the N8 from Veurne to ***Ypres*** *(Ieper).*

Known to British 'Tommies' in World War I as 'Wipers', this glorious 1,000-year-old Gothic drapers' town was completely rebuilt after that terrible conflict. Everything has been painstakingly reconstructed just as it was when it was one of the three great centres of medieval Flemish culture (alongside Bruges and Ghent).

The ultimate symbol of Ypres' weaving-generated wealth was Lakenhalle, the Cloth Halls, a magnificent Gothic extravaganza dating from 1304. Its lovely square Belfort (Belfry) gives a wonderful view over the town – if you don't mind climbing 264 steps. Every three years, on the rather eerie Cats' Festival, stuffed toy cats are thrown from the Belfry while masked 'witches' parade below. Once upon a time the cats were real. The next festival is in 2006.

The town has vowed never to forget the horror of World War I. At the Menin Gate, the names of nearly 55,000 British soldiers are recorded, and the Last Post is sounded every evening at 8.

Take the N8 to ***Menen*** *and on to* ***Kortrijk*** *(Courtrai).*

An emblematic event in Flemish history took place here: the Battle of the Golden Spurs, on 11 July 1302. Flemish peasants, struggling for independence from France, destroyed an army of the flower of French chivalry. After the battle, the Flemish collected over 700 knights' spurs and hung them as a symbol of triumph.

The N34 travels directly from Kortrijk to ***Ghent*** *(Gent).*

The affluent history of Ypres is displayed with this statue placed above the Cloth Halls

On the way, stop off at ***St Martens Latem****, a village of artists and art galleries.*

Ghent, an inland port on the River Scheldt, is generally considered to be the heartland of Flemish culture. It has areas of industrial blight, but the old centre has reminders of its medieval mercantile and weaving traditions, and of the Counts of Flanders, whose capital it was.

The Belfort (Belfry) and Lakenhalle (Cloth Halls) form a complex of 13th- and 14th-century buildings; the 90m-high Belfry offers a superb view over the city. The ostentatious Cloth Halls include an 18th-century prison, source of the legend of the Mammelokker, a young woman whose imprisoned father was starving to death. She supposedly breast-fed him through the bars, on hearing which the authorities freed him.

The bleak Gravensteen (Castle of the Counts), dating from 1180, dominates its surroundings, but gave up its

military role in the 14th century, being used later as a mint, court, gaol and cotton mill.

The Korenlei (Corn Quay) in Ghent is near the centre of the old town

Leaving Ghent on the N9 to Bruges, travel past the towns of Waarschoot and Eeklo to ***Bruges****.*

Bruges, the most charming of all Belgian towns, is described in more detail on pages 76–81. If time is short, simply sit in the delightful Markt (Main Square), at one of the hundreds of café tables.

Continue on the N9 (Ostend direction) until the N377 right turn to ***De Haan****.*

De Haan is one of the few coastal resorts that has not filled up with high-rise apartment blocks. The belle époque mansions that graced the town 100 years ago have been preserved in all their elegance.

Return along the N34 coast road into ***Ostend****.*

What to See in Bruges

Just 25km from Ostend, on the main road (N9) or the motorway (A10), Bruges (Brugge) is a masterpiece of medieval Flemish art and architecture. It has been called the Jewel of Flanders and is a delight of strolling, shopping and sightseeing and unhurried relaxing in pretty squares. Its steeply gabled houses in the old Flemish style, its cobbled streets and its network of canals have incomparable charm, and the centre of the little town can be explored just as well on one of the popular boat tours as by foot.

BEGIJNHOF (BEGUINAGE) ✪

Founded in the 13th century, this charming courtyard of almshouses functioned until recent times as a home for *begijns*, religious lay women akin to nuns. The Begijnhof is now a Benedictine convent. It lies a few hundred metres south of the town centre, and is as pleasing for its riverside setting as for its own quiet beauty. The walk there, too, via the museums, is one of the most satisfying in town. The journey can also be made by horse-drawn carriage. Beyond the Begijnhof, a delightful path continues under lime trees alongside the canal, where swans glide on the dark water.

750m southwest of Markt
Apr–Sep Mon–Fri 10:30–12, 1:45–5:30; Sun 10:45–12, 1:45–6. Oct–Mar opens 30 mins later, closes 30 mins earlier
Good
Cheap

ARENTS HUIS (BRANGWYN MUSEUM) ✪

Works by the English (but Bruges-born) painter and engraver Frank Brangwyn, an apprentice of William Morris, are displayed on the upper floor of this fine 18th-century house. Downstairs are collections of local lacework and Bruges landscape paintings.

400m south of Markt
Dijver 16
050 33 99 11/050 44 87 63
Tue–Sat 9:30–5
None
Cheap

BURG (BURG SQUARE) ✪✪✪

Together in this small space are magnificent buildings that span the centuries from the 14th to the 19th. Pride of place belongs to the Romanesque Heilig Bloed Baziliek (Basilica of the Holy Blood), which contains a much-venerated Relic of the Holy Blood. The Stadhuis (Town Hall) dates from the 14th century, in Gothic style. Other notable buildings are the 16th-century Flemish Renaissance-style Oude Griffie (Old Recorders' House), the 17th-century baroque Proosdij (Deanery) and the 18th-century neo-classical Gerechtshof (Court of Justice).

80 1A

A model member of the Benedictine community looks out of the Begijnhop convent

DIJVER ✪✪

Running along the south side of the main canal, this fine old street combines with Rozenhoedkaai and Steenhouwersdijk to make a wonderful, quiet waterside walk with some of the best views in town, beside the rippling reflections of the Flemish gables.

GROENINGEMUSEUM ✪✪

The Fine Arts Museum houses an important collection of works by the so-called 'Flemish Primitives', including Jan van Eyck, Hans Memling and Rogier van der Weyden.

400m south of Markt
Dijver 12
050 44 87 11
Tue–Sat 9:30–5
Good · Moderate

GROENE REI ✪

At the far end of Steenhouwersdijk, the Groene Rei quayside is the setting for De Pelikaan, an 18th-century charity hospital, one of several distinctive rows of low brick almshouses, built in Bruges by the craft guilds. This one bears the emblem of a pelican.

1.2km southeast of Markt

GRUUTHUSEMUSEUM ✪✪

The fairy-tale edifice of the Gruuthusemuseum was a palace of the Lords of Gruuthuse in the 15th century. This family had the monopoly on the sale of *gruut*, a herbs-and-spices mixture for improving the taste of beer.

400m south of Markt
Dijver 17
050 44 87 62
Tue–Sat 9:30–5
None · Moderate

HUIDENVETTERSPLEIN ✪✪

This atmospheric square is surrounded by café terraces and restaurants, one of which used to be the Tanners' Guild House. Street artists congregate here in good weather to sketch customers sunning themselves on the terrace.

300m southeast of Markt

JERUZALEMKERK ✪

This 15th-century church topped with an unusual lantern tower is supposedly modelled on the Church of the Holy Sepulchre in Jerusalem. Impressive 16th-century stained-glass depicts members of the Adornes family, the Ghent merchants who built the church.

80 2B
Jeruzalemstraat

KANTCENTRUM (LACE CENTRE) ✪✪

Beside the Jeruzalemkerk, in almshouses that once belonged to it, the Bruges Lace Centre tells the story of the city's product, and gives a chance to see it being made. Bruges developed bobbin-lace in the Middle Ages and throughout the 17th century it held the premier position as the leader of fashion and elegance. Even today, Bruges lace is among the most highly valued in the world. The Lace Centre organises classes, shows, exhibitions and demonstrations of traditional and modern lace-making.

80 2B
Peperstraat 3
050 33 00 72
Mon–Sat 10–12, 2–6 (5 on Sat)
Good
Cheap

KRUISPOORT ✪

The waterside district of Kruispoort, northeast of Markt (see below) and near the Jeruzalemkerk and Kantcentrum, has many sights of interest. These include remnants of the ramparts, three windmills and the Engels Klooster (English Convent), with its domed chapel.

80 2C

MARKT ✪✪✪

This superb square, with medieval banners floating from its gabled buildings, is dominated by the Belfort (Belfry), whose 47-bell carillon breaks into song at every

80 1A

opportunity. Below the Belfry are the Hallen, once used for fairs. The nearby, ornate Provinciaal Hof houses the West Flanders provincial government.

500m south of Markt
Mariastraat 38
050 44 87 11/050 33 99 11
Apr–Sep daily 9:30–5; Oct–Mar Thu–Tue 9:30–12:30, 2–5
None
Moderate

MEMLINGMUSEUM ✪✪

The main attraction here is the collection of work by 15th-century artist Hans Memling. His most acclaimed paintings are displayed, including the *Adoration of the Magi*, the *Reliquary of Ursula*, *The Mystic Marriage of St Catherine* and others. The museum is housed in the 12th-century St John's Hospital, and also serves as a hospital museum.

MINNEWATER ✪✪

The pretty banks of the old Minnewater harbour, or Lake of Love, just beyond the Begijnhof, are a favourite spot for picnics or walks. There's an attractive lockhouse, as well as remnants of the old fortifications, and you will always find a group of swans gliding along the waters.

80 2B
Rolweg 40
050 44 87 11
Tue–Sat 9:30–5
Good
Cheap

MUSEUM VOOR FOLKSKUNDE (FOLKLORE MUSEUM) ✪

Preserving the traditions of the last three centuries in West Flanders, this museum occupies former almshouses, and is entered through a café called Zwarte Kat (The Black Cat). It contains reconstructed interiors of a home and a shop.

800m south of Markt
Mariastraat
050 34 53 14
Apr–Sep Mon–Sat 10–12, 2–5, Sun 2–5; Oct–Mar Mon–Fri 10–12, Sat 10–12, 2–4, Sun 2–4
Good Cheap

ONZE-LIEVE-VROUWEKERK (CHURCH OF OUR BLESSED LADY) ✪✪

Inside the church, behind protective glass, is a Madonna and Child by Michelangelo, one of the few works by the Renaissance master outside Italy. The Carrara marble sculpture is surprisingly small, compared with the way it looks in photographs, but it is spellbindingly beautiful.

SPEIGELREI (MIRROR QUAY) ✪

A few paces north of Markt, this canalside road ends in a little square, where fine 15th-century buildings, the Poortersloge and Tonlieu (tollhouse), can be seen, together with a statue of van Eyck.

80 2B
St Annakerkstraat
None

SINT ANNAKERK (CHURCH OF ST ANNE) ✪

A plain brick exterior belies the gaudy Gothic and baroque luxury inside this 17th-century church in the quieter streets northeast of Markt.

250m southwest of Markt
Zuidzandstraat
Mon–Fri 2–5 Sun 3–5. Closed Sun Oct–Mar
Good

ST SALVATORSKATHEDRAAL (ST SAVIOUR'S CATHEDRAL) ✪✪✪

The Gothic tower of this majestic brick edifice, with its neo-Romanesque cap, is one of three which dominate the centre of Bruges (the other two are the Belfry and Onze-Lieve-Vrouwekerk). Inside, the cathedral displays distinguished examples of Flemish painting, sculpture and tapestry.

When in Bruges, don't miss the 79m-high Belfry on the Markt

VISMARKT (FISH MARKET) ✪

Fish are still sold on most mornings in the colonnaded arcade of the Fish Market, which dates from 1821.

300m east of Markt

Excursions from Bruges

BOUDEWIJNPARK ✪

An exciting and enjoyable family leisure attraction near Bruges, featuring a popular Dolphinarium and Seal Island, as well as an Olympic ice rink, a swimming pool, an art gallery and such entertainments as a Haunted Castle, Bambinoland, a Fishing Village Adventure and a skating show called Fantasy on Ice.

Avenue De Baeckestraat 12, St Michiels
050 38 38 38
Jul–Aug daily 10–6; Apr–Jun 10:30–5 (till 6 weekends); Sep open occasionally
Limited
Very expensive

DAMME ✪✪

One of the town's most popular outings is by horse-drawn carriage or (better) along the river to Damme, 7km from Bruges. This historic little waterside town was once a Bruges river port, becoming a separate entity in the Middle Ages. Much survives from that prosperous time. Marktplein, the central square, is typical old Flanders, with its gabled houses and ornate Town Hall. One of the most handsome buildings is the Huyse de Grote Sterre, a 15th-century nobleman's home, which now accommodates the tourist office.

A Walk Around Bruges

Distance
3km

Time
2–3 hours

Start Point
Markt

End Point
Burg

Lunch
Several modest eating places along the route

This walk takes you to some of the lesser-known corners of the town. Walking in the more everyday, less visited district north of the Markt, you get a good feel for the 'real' Bruges, which few tourists see. Here, too, there is grandeur and evocative reminders of the past, while ordinary bars and restaurants along the way cater mainly for locals.

Leave the Markt along Philipstockstraat. Turn left into Cordoeaniersstraat to St Janplein. On the other side, take St Jansstraat to St Maartensplen.

The interesting baroque church of Sint-Walburgakerk is found here.

Walk along the left side of the church in Hoornstraat to the Verversdijk, then turn right and cross over the bridge to come into St Annakerkstraat.

This street is named after the Church of St Anne, which dates back to the 17th century (➤ 78).

At the back of the church, cross Jeruzalemstraat towards the Jeruzalemkerk on the corner.

Next door to the Jeruzalemkerk is the Kantcentrum (Peperstraat 3), where you can see how lace is made (➤ 77).

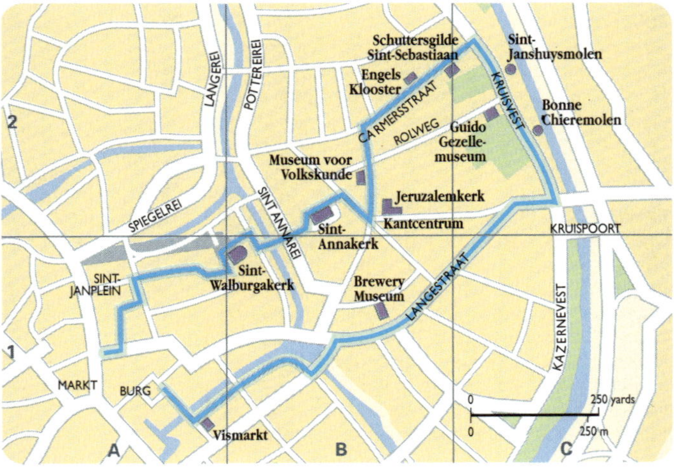

From the Jeruzalemkerk turn into Balstraat and then Rolweg, and the Museum voor Volkskunde. Cross Rolweg to Carmersstraat and turn right.

No 85 is the dome of the Engels Klooster; No 174 is the old Schuttersgilde Sint-Sebastiaan, and straight ahead on Kruisvest is the Sint-Janshuysmolen windmill.

Turn right along Kruisvest.

On the corner with Rolweg is a museum dedicated to the Flemish poet Guido Gezelle (1830–99), and further along, the Bonne Chiere windmill.

At Kruispoort turn right into Langestraat.

At No 47 is the Brewery Museum (entrance at Verbrand Nieuwland 10).

Before the end of the Langestraat, turn left over a bridge into Predikherenstraat, cross another bridge and turn right to Groene Rei.

This is one of Bruges' loveliest corners. At the end of the street is Vismarkt, with a morning fish market held from Tuesday to Saturday (➤ 79).

To the right, an alley under the arch leads to the Burg.

The bridge at Minnewater is one attraction that makes Bruges a great place to explore on foot

What to see in Belgian Flanders

BRUGES (BRUGGE) (➤ 76–81)

DE PANNE ✪✪

28km southwest of Ostend

In addition to the widest beach on the Flemish coast, De Panne has a superb nature reserve of dunes, where sand-loving plants and wildlife thrive. The shoreline here is a world-leading venue for the sport of sand-yachting.

GHENT (GENT) (➤ 74–5, TOUR)

YPRES (IEPER) (➤ 74, TOUR)

KOKSIJDE ✪✪

23km southwest of Ostend

Museum
Kabouterlaan 42
058 52 12 29 · Good

This popular little family resort combines nature and art, with the highest and longest sand dunes on the Belgian coast, as well as a fascinating museum devoted to the surrealist painter, Paul Delvaux.

OOSTDUINKERKE ✪

22km southwest of Ostend

National Museum of Fishing
Pastoor Schmitzstraat 5
058 51 24 68
Daily 10–12, 2–6
Limited. No wheelchairs
Inexpensive

The shrimp-fishermen of this beach resort still use the visually striking traditional method of fishing on horseback, dragging nets through the offshore shallows. On the flat sands, 'landsailing' is popular. In town, the National Museum of Fishing displays fishing boats, equipment and items related to folklore.

OSTEND (OOSTENDE) ✪✪✪

Fine Art Museum
In Stedelijk Feest en Kultuurpaleis, Waponplein
059 80 53 35
Wed–Mon 10–12, 2–5 (winter PM only)
Good
Inexpensive

James Ensor's Home
Vlaanderenstraat 27
059 80 53 35
Jun–Sep, Christmas and Easter hols Mon–Sat 10–12, 2–5; rest of year Sat–Sun only 2–5
None · Inexpensive

Modern Art Museum
Romestraat 11
059 50 81 18
Tue–Sun 10–6
Limited · Moderate

Combining busy ferry port with old-world beach resort, Ostend offers a great variety of entertainment and enjoyment. Stroll along its beaches and fishing quays, where there's a big choice of seafood restaurants – the town is famous for top-quality oysters.

The Fine Arts Museum gives pride of place to James Ensor, the acclaimed Ostend artist whose work led to the development of Surrealism.

James Ensor's Home has been restored and turned into a museum. His studio is on the second floor.

The Modern Art Museum displays Ostend's remarkable collection of 20th-century art, including Expressionism, abstract art and pop-art.

The town's lively casino contains not only gaming rooms but a theatre, art exhibitions and a concert hall, which von Karajan said had the best acoustics in the world. The casino is also the venue for the many Ostend festivals and events, such as the strange Dead Rat Fair, when men dress as masked women, on the first Saturday in March.

VEURNE (FURNES) (➤ 73, TOUR)

Where to Shop

Bruges

There is nowhere easier to shop for Belgium's specialities – chocolates, lace and the local biscuits called *speculoos* – than in Bruges. The town is a shopper's delight, with large and small outlets selling the best of traditional Flemish wares. The town's shopping street, naturally geared more to residents than visitors, is Steenstraat, leading off the main square, Markt.

Ostend

Ostend's main shopping street is Kapellestraat, running from the central square, Wapenplein, to the yacht marina, and some of its neighbouring streets. Familiar fashion chains rub shoulders with specialist stores selling hand-made chocolates, Belgian designer clothes, traditional lace and souvenirs. If you prefer supermarket shopping, visit Delhaze, near the Ostend railway station.

In Bruges Centre

Bottle Shop

Selling over 300 different mineral waters and 500 different beers, this is the best place to find gift tipple.

✉ Wollestraat 13 🕑 Winter 9–7; summer 9AM–11PM

Bruges Diamanthuis

Diamond-polishing has been a Belgian speciality since the Middle Ages – and it all started in Bruges. This shop offers a wide range of diamond jewellery.

✉ Cordoeanierstraat 5
🕑 Mon–Fri 10–12, 1:30–5, Sat 10–3

Claeys

This long established lace shop also organises courses in traditional arts and crafts and stocks some delightful handmade examples.

✉ Katelijnestraat 54
🕑 Daily 9–7

Deldycke

A delicatessen-style food shop selling a tempting array of finest cheeses and *charcuterie* well worth taking home, plus drinks.

✉ Wollestraat 23
🕑 Wed–Mon 9–2, 3–6:30

Depla

Classic Belgian chocolates.

✉ Eekhautstraat 23
🕑 10–6:30

De Striep

Comics and cartoons are another Belgian speciality, and this shop sells a huge range of them.

✉ Katelijnestraat 42
🕑 Tue–Sat 10–12:30, 1:30–7; Mon PM only

Dijver Antiques and Secondhand Market

This canalside market comes close to being a flea market at times, yet some good value antiques can be found.

✉ Dijver
🕑 Apr–Sep, Sat and Sun

Gruuthuse

High-quality lace, including antique – all guaranteed Belgian.

✉ Dijver 15
🕑 10–6:30, till 7 in summer

L'Heroïne

For chic fashions and accessories; L'Heroïne specialises in Belgian designers.

✉ Noordzandstraat 32
🕑 Mon–Sat 10–6:30

Pralinette

Enter a delectable world of freshly-made chocolate at the largest praline shop in Bruges, where cauldrons of melting chocolate increase the temptation.

✉ Wollestraat 31b 🕑 10–7

Ostend

Leonidas

The ubiquitous budget praline chain sells popular chocolates at around half the price of some of the shop's top of the range neighbours. Ideal for gifts for the office.

✉ Kapellestraat 9 ☎ 059 80 50 34 🕑 Daily 9:30–6:30

Neuhaus

Neuhaus in Brussels invented the classic Belgian chocolate in the 19th century. Here the chocolatier's favourites, including the nougat-filled Caprice, are sold.

✉ Koningsstraat 6 ☎ 059 50 52 63 🕑 Tue–Sat 9:30–6:30, Sun 9:30–noon

Where to Eat & Drink

Belgian food is of a generally high standard, and the country has more Michelin-starred restaurants per head than France. In addition, portions tend to be generous. As for bars and brasseries, the choice is overwhelming. As well as scores of local beers, invariably hearty snacks and meals are available.

Bruges

Markt, the handsome main square with its massive brick belfry, is a focal point for bars and popular low-cost eating places. Here, a dozen or so bar-restaurants have put out their tables and serve inexpensive three-course set meals – typically consisting of a soup,followed by mussels and a dessert.

Breydel de Coninck (€–€€)
A popular mussel restaurant, regarded as the best by many locals, even though the décor is rather dull and somewhat uninspiring.
✉ Breidelstraat 24 ☎ 50 33 97 46 🕐 Closed Wed, Jun

Chez Olivier (€€–€€€)
Cosy restaurant in an old house, with views over one of the prettiest canals, serving stylish French fare.
✉ Meestraat 9 ☎ 50 33 36 59 🕐 Closed Thu, Fri lunch

Chagall (€–€€)
A cosy bar-restaurant serving a range of Belgian specialities, such as eel, ribsteaks and mussels, served to the accompaniment of classical music. Good choice for a coffee during the day or a liqueur after dinner.
✉ Sint-Amandstraat 40 ☎ 50 33 61 12 🕐 Open all year

Den Gouden Harynck (€€–€€€)
A Michelin-starred chef prepares the freshest ingredients, without too many frills. Specialities include some pleasant surprises like smoked lobster with fig chutney or scallops with goose liver. Typically Brugean décor.
✉ Groeninge 25 ☎ 50 33 76 37 🕐 Closed Sun, Mon

De Karmeliet (€€€)
Often regarded by many as Bruges' best restaurant. De Karmeliet offers inspired and creative Belgian cuisine, prepared by expert chef Geert Van Hecke and served in the stylish high-ceilinged rooms of an old mansion house.
✉ Langestraat 19 ☎ 50 33 82 59 🕐 Mon–Sat lunch, dinner; Sun lunch. Closed Mon

De Lotus (€)
A rarity this, a vegetarian restaurant that attracts non-veggies to the tables! Good value set menu.
✉ Wapenmakersstraat 5 ☎ 50 33 10 78 🕐 Mon–Sat 11:30–2PM, Thur–Sat 7PM–late

De Snippe (€€€)
Popular restaurant in a well-restored 18th-century house. The chef Luc Huysentruyt, a disciple of Escoffier and a Master Chef of Belgium, loves innovation, but his cuisine is strongly rooted in tradition. His specialities are amazing fish dishes.
✉ Nieuwe Gentweg 53 ☎ 50 33 70 70 🕐 Tue–Sat lunch, dinner, Mon dinner. Closed Sun, Mon lunch

De Vlissinghe (€€)
Reputedly the oldest café in Bruges, built around 1515. The delightful 17th-century room has been used in films. Popular with locals, as well as visitors.
✉ Blekerstraat 2 ☎ 50 34 37 37 🕐 Wed, Sat 2PM–1AM, Mon, Thu, Fri 4PM–1AM, Sun 11:30AM–9PM. Closed Tue

De Witte Poorte (€€€)
Renowned for its gourmet Belgian cuisine in the warm atmosphere of a large room under rustic medieval vaults.
✉ Jan van Eyck Plain 6 ☎ 50 33 08 83 🕐 Closed Mon, Sat

Ganzespel (€–€€)
Typical Flemish daily specialities in a convivial atmosphere. Light snacks and pasta options for the budget conscious.
✉ Ganzestraat 37 ☎ 50 33 12 33 🕐 Wed–Sun 12–2, 6–10

Heer Halewijn (€€)
A great place to sit by the fire in winter and taste some excellent wine with

farmhouse cheeses or grills.
Walplein 10
50 33 92 20 **Dinner only. Closed Mon, Tue**

Pandreitje (€€€)
Much-lauded restaurant with excellent fish specialities, particularly a fish pie of smoked eel. There are *dégustation* menus or à la carte dishes, served in the plush interior or in the lovely garden in summer.
Pandreitje 6 **50 33 11 90**
Closed Sun, Wed

Trium Trattoria (€)
The best Italian restaurant in Bruges with fresh pasta and pizzas served by some of the most charming waiters outside Italy.
Academiestraat 23
50 33 30 60 **Tue–Thu 9–8, Fri–Sun 9–9. Closed Mon**

't Brugs Beertje
The place for the true beer-lover with a selection of over 300 traditionally brewed Belgian beers, each served in its special glass. The atmosphere is as Belgian as it can be, and the landlord will be happy to choose a beer to suit your personality. Many beers are rare and only on sale here.
Kemelstraat 5 **50 33 96 16** **4PM–1AM; closed Wed**

Ostend

Choose from a wide range of waterfront restaurants on Ostend's Visserskai (Fishing Quay) that serve up fish and shellfish as fresh as it gets. Outside, on the quay, stallholders sell the freshly caught seafood.

Ghent

Look around the central Botermarkt for good places to eat. One of the best is the beautiful 13th-century **Cours St Georges** (Botermarkt 2, 9224 24 24, open for lunch and dinner, closed Sun), with a range of good French and Flemish dishes. If you just want a drink, Ghent's town centre has over 300 bars, including one specialising in *geniuhre*, the Belgian gin, called **Dreupelkot**. (Groentenmarkt 12).

Where to Stay

Bruges

Die Swaene (€€€)
One of Bruges' most romantic hotels, offering beautiful rooms furnished with plenty of lace and (some) with canal views. Although central, it is still pleasingly quiet, and with good, attentive service.
Steenhouwersdijk 1 (Groene Rei) **50 34 27 98**

Duc de Bourgogne (€€)
Has a slightly aged feel but comfortable rooms in the heart of Bruges, overlooking one of the most picturesque canals. The stylish restaurant serves excellent Belgian cuisine (closed Mon and Tue lunch).
Huidenvettersplein 12
50 33 20 38

Grand Hôtel du Sablon (€€)
A traditional, city-centre hotel with a beautiful stained-glass dome in art-nouveau style over the lobby. The rear part of the hotel was an inn 400 years ago, but its rooms now offer all the modern conveniences you would expect.
Noordzandstraat 21
50 33 39 02

Prinsenhof (€€)
You'll find suprisingly moderate prices and a reliably warm welcome at this grand town-centre mansion, which was once a nobleman's home. Behind the brick façade, there are large, beautifully furnished rooms.
Ontvangersstraat 9
50 34 26 90

Ostend

NH Oostende (€€–€€€)
Formerly the well-known Royal Astor, this stylish renovated three-star hotel is close to the town centre, casino and beach. It offers modern, spacious rooms and a wide range of facilities, including a good restaurant.
Herstraat 15 **59 80 37 73**

Ghent

Sint Jorishof (€€)
Europe's oldest hotel dates from 1228. Newer rooms have been converted from 19th-century homes of the nobility. The restaurant is first class.
Botermarkt 2 **92 24 24 24** **Closed Wed, plus Tue in winter**

WHAT YOU NEED

● Required
○ Suggested
▲ Not required

Some countries require a passport to remain valid for a minimum period (usually at least six months) beyond the date of entry – contact the consulate or embassy or your travel agent for details.

	France	Belgium
Passport/National Identity Card	●	●
Visa (regulations can change – check before booking your trip)	▲	▲
Onward or Return Ticket	▲	▲
Health Inoculations	▲	▲
Health Documentation (reciprocal agreement document) (➤ 91, Health)	●	●
Travel Insurance	○	○
Driving Licence (national)	●	●
Car Insurance Certificate (if own car)	○	○
Car Registration Document (if own car)	●	●

WHEN TO GO

Average figures for Caen

High season

Low season

7°C	8°C	12°C	13°C	17°C	20°C	22°C	22°C	20°C	15°C	11°C	8°C
JAN	FEB	MAR	APR	MAY	JUN	JUL	AUG	SEP	OCT	NOV	DEC

Very wet Wet Cloud Sun Sun/ Showers

TOURIST OFFICES IN BRITAIN

- French Tourist Office
  ✉ 178 Piccadilly, London W1V 0AL
  ☎ 0906 824 4123 (premium rate); fax: 020 7493 6594; www.franceguide.com
- Tourism Flanders-Brussels
  ✉ 31 Pepper Street London E14 9RW
  ☎ 0906 3020245 (premium rate); www.visitflanders.co.uk

TOURIST OFFICES ABROAD

IN FRANCE:

Boulogne
Office de Tourisme
✉ 24 quai Gambetta
☎ 03 21 10 88 10; www.tourisme-boulognesurmer.com

Calais
- Office de Tourisme
  ✉ 12 boulevard Clémenceau
  ☎ 03 21 96 62 40; www.ot-calais.fr

Cherbourg
- Office de Tourisme
  ✉ 2 quai Alexandre III
  ☎ 02 33 93 52 02; www.ot-cherbourg-contentin.fr

Dieppe
- Office de Tourisme
  ✉ Pont Jehan d'Ango
  ☎ 02 32 14 40 60; www.dieppetourisme.com

IN BELGIUM:

Bruges
- VVV/Toerisme Brugge
  ✉ Burg 11
  ☎ 050 44 86 86; www.bugge.be

Ostend
- Promotie Toerisme
  ✉ Monacoplein 2
  ☎ 059 70 11 99; www.oostende.be/home.htm

ARRIVING

Hoverspeed (Dover–Calais, Newhaven–Dieppe) 0870 240 8070; www.hoverspeed.com
Eurotunnel (Folkestone–Calais) 08000 969 992; www.eurotunnel.com
P&O Ferries (Dover–Calais, Portsmouth–Cherbourg, Portsmouth–Le-Havre 08705 202020; www.poferries.com
Sea France (Dover–Calais) 08705 711 711; www.seafrance.fr
Brittan Ferries (Poole–Cherbourg, Portsmouth–Caen) 08703 665 333; www.brittanyferries.com
Speedferries (Dover–Boulogne); www.speedferries.com

TIME

France and Belgium are one hour ahead of UK time throughout the year (sometimes excepting a March or October week when British and European clocks are changed on different dates).

CUSTOMS

YES

From another EU country for personal use (guidelines):
800 cigarettes, 200 cigars,
1 kilogram of tobacco
10 litres of spirits (over 22%)
20 litres of aperitifs
90 litres of wine, of which 60 litres can be sparkling wine
110 litres of beer

From a non-EU country for your personal use, the allowances are:
200 cigarettes OR
50 cigars OR 20 grams of tobacco
1 litre of spirits (over 22%)
2 litres of intermediary products (e.g. sherry) and sparkling wine
2 litres of still wine
50 grams of perfume
0.25 litres of eau de toilette
The value limit for goods is 175 euros

Travellers under 17 years of age are not entitled to the tobacco and alcohol allowances

NO

Drugs, firearms, ammunition, offensive weapons, obscene material, unlicensed animals.

MONEY

The euro is the official currency of France and Belgium. Euro notes are issued in denominations of 5, 10, 20, 50, 100, 200 and 500 euros. Coins are issued in denominations of 1 and 2 euros and 1, 2, 5, 20 and 50 cents; 100 cents = €1.
Travellers' cheques and cash can be changed at most banks. Visa, Access and MasterCard are generally accepted in hotels and restaurants. ATMs (cash machines) are widely available: they issue local currency drawn on your UK credit card or bank account.

PHOTOGRAPHY

What to photograph: the coast, with its broad sands and beautiful light; rural villages and timber-framed houses; abbey and château ruins.
Restrictions: some museums will allow you to photograph inside. In churches with frescoes and icons prior permission is required for flashlight.
Where to buy film: the most popular brands and types of film can be bought from shops and photo laboratories. Film development is quite expensive.

PERSONAL SAFETY

In France:
The *Police Municipale* (blue uniforms) carry out police duties in cities and towns. The *Gendarmes* (blue trousers, black jackets, white belts), the national police force, cover the countryside and smaller places. The CRS deal with emergencies and also look after safety on beaches.

In Belgium:
There are two main police branches: the *Police/Politie*, ordinary local police; and the *Gendarmerie/Rijkswacht*, who handle serious crime.

All the French and Belgian towns included here are generally very safe, with low crime levels. However, it is wise to take certain precautions:

- Do not use unmanned roadside rest areas at night.
- Cars, especially foreign cars, should be secured.
- In crowded places, beware of pickpockets.

	France	Belgium
Police	**17**	**101**
Fire	**18**	**100**
Ambulance	**15**	**100**

TELEPHONES

With few exceptions, public phones in both France and Belgium require a pre-paid phone card (available from newsagents and other shops).

To call the UK from either country, the international dialling code is 00 44.

Calling from the UK, the code for Belgium is 00 32, for France, 00 33.

NATIONAL HOLIDAYS

In France and Belgium

1 Jan	New Year's Day
Mar/Apr	Easter Monday
1 May	Labour Day
8 May	VE Day
May	Ascension
May/Jun	Pentecost (Whit Monday)
11 Jul	Flemish Community Day (Belgium only)
14 Jul	National Day (France only)
21 Jul	National Day (Belgium only)
15 Aug	Assumption
1 Nov	All Saints
11 Nov	Armistice Day
25 Dec	Christmas

Where national holidays fall on a Sunday, the next day is taken as a holiday instead.

TIPS/GRATUITIES

Yes ✓ No ✕	France		Belgium
Restaurants (service included; tip optional)	✕		✕
Cafés (service included; tip optional)	✕		✕
Hotels (service included; tip optional)	✕		✕
Hairdressers	✓	(€1/2)	✕
Taxis	✕		✕
Tour guides	✓	(€1/2)	✕
Cinema usherettes	✕		✕
Porters	✓	(€1/2)	✕
Cloakroom attendants	✓	(small)	✓
Toilets	✓	(small)	✓

In France, service is usually included in restaurants, cafés, bars and hotels. Tips of €1 or€2 are expected for hairdressers and tour guides; and small change is expected for cloakroom attendants and toilet attendants.

In Belgium, tipping is not usual (except for an optional rounding up of bills with small change). Even taxis do not expect a tip. However, attendants at public toilets should be paid a small fee.

WEIGHTS AND MEASURES

Conversion Table

From	To	Multiply by	From	To	Multiply by
Inches	Centimetres	2.54	Gallons	Litres	4.5460
Feet	Metres	0.3048	Ounces	Grams	28.35
Yards	Metres	0.9144	Pounds	Grams	453.6
Miles	Kilometres	1.6090	Pounds	Kilograms	0.4536
Acres	Hectares	0.4047	Tons	Tonnes	1.0160

To convert back, for example from centimetres to inches, divide by the number in the third column.

LANGUAGE

In France, it's helpful to know some basic French. In Belgian Flanders, English is widely spoken. Ostend and Bruges, and all of Belgium except Brussels and the Ardennes province in the east, are Flemish-speaking. German is also widely spoken throughout Belgium.

	ENGLISH	FRENCH	DUTCH	GERMAN
NUMBERS	one	*un/une*	*één*	*eins*
	two	*deux*	*twee*	*zwei*
	three	*trois*	*drie*	*drei*
	four	*quatre*	*vier*	*vier*
	five	*cinq*	*vijf*	*fünf*
	six	*six*	*zes*	*sechs*
	seven	*sept*	*zeven*	*sieben*
	eight	*huit*	*acht*	*acht*
	nine	neuf	*negen*	*neun*
	ten	dix	*tien*	*zehn*
DAYS OF THE WEEK	Monday	*Lundi*	*Maandag*	*Montag*
	Tuesday	*Mardi*	*Dinsdag*	*Dienstag*
	Wednesday	*Mercredi*	*Woensdag*	*Mittwoch*
	Thursday	*Jeudi*	*Donderdag*	*Donnerstag*
	Friday	*Vendredi*	*Vrijdag*	*Freitag*
	Saturday	*Samedi*	*Zaterdag*	*Samstag*
	Sunday	*Dimanche*	*Zondag*	*Sonntag*
USEFUL PHRASES	good morning	*bonjour*	*goedemorgen*	*guten tag*
	good afternoon	*bonjour*	*goedemiddag*	*guten tag*
	good evening	*bon soir*	*goedenavond*	*guten abend*
	goodbye	*au revoir*	*tot ziens*	*auf wiedersehen*
	please	*s'il vous plaît*	*alstublieft*	*bitte*
	thank you	*merci*	*dank u wel*	*danke schön*
	yes	*oui*	*ja*	*ja*
	no	*non*	*neen*	*nein*
	how much?	*combien?*	*hoeveel?*	*wieviel?*
	excuse me	*pardon*	*pardon*	*bitte*
	sorry	*excusez-moi*	*pardon*	*tut mir leid*

PUBLIC TRANSPORT

Every channel port has a bus service stopping at bus stops on main roads within the town centre and to outlying districts. Pay fares on boarding to the driver. Within town, fares are inexpensive and services frequent from about 7AM to 7PM. Out of town bus services are geared towards getting people to and from work in the morning and evening. However, there are frequent buses from Calais to Cité de l'Europe and from Ostend to Bruges. In addition trains run several times daily between Calais and Boulogne, between Calais and Lille, and between Ostend and Bruges. In Lille, an excellent bus service is supplemented by a modern driverless metro.

CONCESSIONS

In both France and Belgium, most concessions for young or older people are for locals only. However, a student card or proof of age under 26, or over 60, often allows discounted entry to many museums, attractions, entertainments etc. Ask at tourist offices for information on other concessions for young or older people or for people with disabilities.

TAXIS

Taxis pick up at taxi ranks at railway stations, ferry terminals and airports. Hotels and restaurants can usually give a taxi call number. Check the taxi has a meter; there is a pick-up charge, plus a rate per minute. Note that in Belgium drivers are not allowed to stop if you are less than 100m from a taxi rank.

CAR RENTAL

All large towns have car-rental agencies at airports and railway stations. Car hire can be expensive although some tour operators offer packages which work out cheaper than hiring locally.

CLOTHING SIZES

France	UK	Belgium		
46	36	46	36	Suits
48	38	48	38	Suits
50	40	50	40	Suits
52	42	52	42	Suits
54	44	54	44	Suits
56	46	56	46	Suits
41	7	41	8	Shoes
42	7.5	42	8.5	Shoes
43	8.5	43	9.5	Shoes
44	9.5	44	10.5	Shoes
45	10.5	45	11.5	Shoes
46	11	46	12	Shoes
37	14.5	37	14.5	Shirts
38	15	38	15	Shirts
39/40	15.5	39/40	15.5	Shirts
41	16	41	16	Shirts
42	16.5	42	16.5	Shirts
43	17	43	17	Shirts
36	8	34	6	Dresses
38	10	36	8	Dresses
40	12	38	10	Dresses
42	14	40	12	Dresses
44	16	42	14	Dresses
46	18	44	16	Dresses
38	4.5	38	6	Shoes
38	5	38	6.5	Shoes
39	5.5	39	7	Shoes
39	6	39	7.5	Shoes
40	6.5	40	8	Shoes
41	7	41	8.5	Shoes

ELECTRICITY

The power supply in France and Belgium is 220 volts.

Type of socket: round two-hole sockets taking two round-pin (or occasionally three round-pin) plugs. British visitors should bring an adapter.

OPENING HOURS – FRANCE

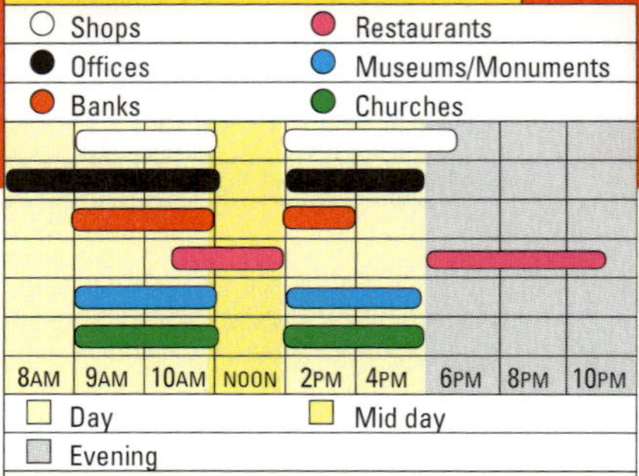

France

In addition to the times shown above, afternoon time of shops in summer can extend in the most popular centres. Most shops close Sunday and many on Monday. Small food shops open from 7AM and may open Sunday morning. Large department stores do not close for lunch and hypermarkets open 10AM to 9 or 10PM, but may shut Monday morning. Banks are closed Sunday as well as Saturday or Monday. Museums and monuments have extended summer hours. Many close one day a week; either Monday (municipal ones) or Tuesday (national ones).

OPENING HOURS – BELGIUM

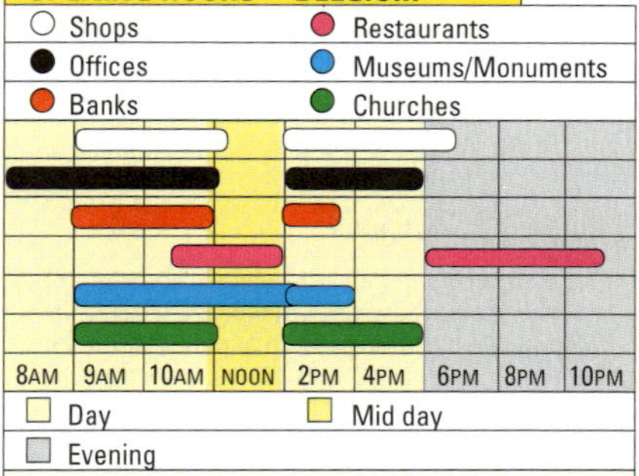

Belgium

Shops are usually open from 9 to 6 or 7 (there is no official closing time). Many shops in Bruges, fewer in Brussels, close for lunch (usually 12:30–2). Supermarkets and some grocery stores stay open until 9PM. The main shopping streets and areas have late shopping one night a week, usually Friday, until 9PM. Banks open at 9AM and close between 3:30 and 5; some close for lunch. Offices sometimes close early on Friday afternoons. Post offices open from 9 to 5, although the main office stays open later. Museums: phone first as opening hours vary. Most open 9–4. In Brussels museums generally close on Monday, in Bruges on Tuesday. Some close for lunch, and some are open longer hours in the summer.

HEALTH

Insurance

Nationals of EU and some other countries can get medical treatment in France and Belguim at reduced cost on production of a qualifying form (Form E111 for Britons), although private medical insurance is advised and is essential for other visitors.

Pharmacies

Recognised by their green cross sign – have highly qualified staff able to offer medical advice, provide first aid and prescribe and provide a wide range of drugs, though some are available by prescription (*ordonnance*) only.

DRIVING

From the point of view of both safety and the law, motoring in France and Belgium have almost exactly the same requirements. Driving is pleasant and easy on the excellent road network on both sides of the border. Law enforcement however, is perfunctory and severe. Remember that visitors bringing vehicles into France and Belgium are required to display the appropriate nationality sticker of the country of origin.

Documents

Insurance certificate, original car registration documentation and your driving licence must always be carried when driving. A full UK driving licence is required by British motorists. The minimum driving age for a car or motorcycle is 18.

Insurance

Third party motor insurance is compulsory. Comprehensive insurance issued by UK insurers is valid in the EU (a Green Card is no longer required, although some insurers wish to be informed that you are going abroad). Make sure too that you have adequate vehicle breakdown protection and personal travel insurance.

Lights

When driving on the right the headlamps of right-hand drive vehicles should be altered to avoid dazzling on-coming vehicles. Easily fitted headlamp converter kits are available from motor accessory shops. Dipped lights must be used in rain and poor visibility, as well as after dark. As a general rule motorcyclists must use a dipped headlight at all times.

Penalties

Most minor offences, including speeding, not stopping at a Stop sign, overtaking where forbidden and not wearing a seat belt, are punishable by an immediate on-the-spot fine (up to €160 in France). Issuing a receipt is part of the procedure – always be sure to get one, and keep it carefully. More serious motoring offences, such as drink-driving, are liable to impounding of the car, heavy fines or imprisonment.

In town centres, cars parked in no-parking zones are generally towed away. Kerbside signs always make it clear what the parking regulations are in each street.

Roads

Out-of-town highways are generally well-maintained. Roads in town may be of poorer standard, and are often cobbled. Some country lanes may also be poor. However, there is relatively little traffic out of town in the French and Belgian Channel coastal area.

Motorways (A) are called *autoroutes* in French, *snelweg* in Flemish.

In France, tolls are charged on most motorways except where they encircle towns. Other exceptions include quite long stretches of the A26 inland from Calais and the A16 Channel coast motorway between Dunkerque and Calais and Boulogne. Motorways are toll-free throughout the area of Belgium covered by this book.

Main roads (N or RN) are called *routes nationales* in France, *routes principales* (French) or *hoofdverbindingsweg* (Flemish) in Belgium.

Secondary roads (D in France, N in Belgium) are called *routes départementales* in France, *routes régionales* (French) or *secundaire verbindingsweg* (Flemish) in Belgium. The extensive network of clearly marked, straight, well-maintained D roads in France makes it easy to avoid busy main highways.

Drinking and driving

In both France and Belgium, the maximum legal level of alcohol in the blood is 0.05 per cent. According to the amount of excess level, penalties range from on-the-spot fines, impounding the vehicle, confiscation of driving licence etc up to prison sentences of varying severity.

Children in cars

In France, children under 10 are not allowed to travel in the front seats (except for babies up to nine months weighing under 9kg and seated in a rear-facing baby seat). In Belgium, children under 12 may not sit in the front unless using seat belts or child restraint appropriate to size and weight. In France and Belgium, children seated in the rear must use an appropriate restraint system if fitted.

Rules of the Road

Drive on the right and always give way to anything approaching from the right except:
- where your road has *passage protégé* (indicated by a rectangular yellow sign – take care where you see a sign showing the yellow rectangle crossed out, meaning that you no longer have priority over traffic from the right)
- where vehicles coming from the right are emerging from private property
- where other signs indicate that you have a priority

This rule, known as *priorité à droite*, may take the unwary by surprise, especially in town centres, where traffic coming from side roads on your right will drive out as if it has a 'green light', even if you are on a main road.

Most roundabouts now give priority to vehicles already on the roundabout. In France, on approaching these roundabouts you will see signs saying *Vous n'avez pas la priorité* and/or *Cedez le passage*. In Belgium, a red triangular Give Way sign is used. If there are no such signs, the usual priority rule applies, so traffic already on the roundabout has to give way to traffic entering it. (Remember to go round the roundabout in an anti-clockwise direction!)

Seat belts

Seat belts must be worn at all times in both the front and the back of the car, except in older vehicles which do not have seat belts fitted.

Safe motoring
- Equip your vehicle with a warning triangle
- Spectacle-wearers should carry a spare set
- It is wise to carry spare bulbs for the lights
- Ensure tyres are in good condition and properly inflated. If they are worn down to below 2mm of tread or likely to be before you get back, replace them before you leave
- Motorcyclists and their pillion passengers must wear crash helmets
- Take extra care when overtaking – driving on the right with a right-hand drive makes it difficult to see oncoming traffic

Speed limits

Generally the speed limit in Belgian and French built-up areas is 50kph (31mph), but watch for signs.

In France limits are 90kph (55mph) outside built-up areas, 110kph (68mph) on dual carriageways and 130kph (80mph) on motorways except where signposted otherwise; lower limits of 80kph (49mph) , 100 kph (62mph) and 110kph (68mph) respectively apply in wet weather and to drivers who have held a licence for less than two years. A minimum speed of 80kph (49mph) applies in the fast lane on level stretches of French motorways during good daytime visibility.

In Belgium limits are 90kph (55mph) outside built-up areas and 120kph (74mph) on dual carriageways separated by a central reservation and motorways. A minimum speed of 70kph (43mph) applies on Belgian motorways.

Valuables

Crime is not a major problem in the areas covered by this book, but it would be wise put valuables out of sight when leaving your car parked.

Petrol, tolls and payment

Regular unleaded petrol (*essence sans plomb*), high-octane unleaded (*super sans plomb*) and diesel (*gasoil* or *diesel*) are widely available. Lead replacement petrol (LRP) is known in France as *super carburant* or *super ARS*. Petrol prices are a little higher than in the UK, except for diesel, which is much cheaper.

Credit cards are widely accepted at petrol stations. UK cards are valid but some card reading machines may have difficulty in reading them. If you have any queries regarding this, contact your card issuer. Credit cards can be used to pay motorway tolls; usually no signature is required. Travellers' cheques cannot usually be used to pay for petrol, and are not accepted at motorway toll-booths.

Dear Essential Traveller

Your comments, opinions and recommendations are very important to us. So please help us to improve our travel guides by taking a few minutes to complete this simple questionnaire.

You do not need a stamp (unless posted outside the UK). If you do not want to cut this page from your guide, then photocopy it or write your answers on a plain sheet of paper.

Send to: **The Editor, AA World Travel Guides, FREEPOST SCE 4598, Basingstoke RG21 4GY.**

Your recommendations...

We always encourage readers' recommendations for restaurants, nightlife or shopping – if your recommendation is used in the next edition of the guide, we will send you a ***FREE*** **AA** ***Essential*** **Guide** of your choice. Please state below the establishment name, location and your reasons for recommending it.

____

____

____

____

Please send me **AA** ***Essential*** ____________________

(see list of titles inside the front cover)

About this guide...

Which title did you buy?

AA *Essential* ____________________

Where did you buy it? ____________________

When? m m / y y

Why did you choose an AA *Essential* Guide? ____________________

____

____

____

____

Did this guide meet your expectations?

Exceeded ☐ Met all ☐ Met most ☐ Fell below ☐

Please give your reasons ____________________

____

____

____

continued on next page...

Were there any aspects of this guide that you particularly liked? ________

____

____

____

Is there anything we could have done better? ________

____

____

____

____

About you...

Name (*Mr/Mrs/Ms*) ________

Address ________

____

________ Postcode ________

Daytime tel nos ________

Which age group are you in?

Under 25 ☐ 25–34 ☐ 35–44 ☐ 45–54 ☐ 55–64 ☐ 65+ ☐

How many trips do you make a year?

Less than one ☐ One ☐ Two ☐ Three or more ☐

Are you an AA member? Yes ☐ No ☐

About your trip...

When did you book? m m / y y When did you travel? m m / y y

How long did you stay? ________

Was it for business or leisure? ________

Did you buy any other travel guides for your trip?

If yes, which ones? ________

____

Thank you for taking the time to complete this questionnaire. Please send it to us as soon as possible, and remember, you do not need a stamp (*unless posted outside the UK*).

Happy Holidays!